YOUTH ACADEMY
TRAINING PROGRAM
U5-8

New Methodology From
Italian Serie 'A' Coaches'

WRITTEN BY

MIRKO MAZZANTINI   &   SIMONE BOMBARDIERI

PUBLISHED BY

YOUTH ACADEMY TRAINING PROGRAM
U5-8

New Methodology From Italian Serie 'A' Coaches'

First Published June 2013 by SoccerTutor.com

Info@soccertutor.com | www.SoccerTutor.com

UK: 0208 1234 007 | **US:** (305) 767 4443 | **ROTW:** +44 208 1234 007

ISBN: 978-0-9576705-0-1

Author
Mirko Mazzantini and Simone Bombardieri © 2013

Edited by
Alex Fitzgerald - SoccerTutor.com

Cover Design by
Alex Macrides, Think Out Of The Box Ltd.
Email: design@thinkootb.com Tel: +44 (0) 208 144 3550

Diagrams
Diagram designs by SoccerTutor.com. All the diagrams in this book have been created using SoccerTutor.com Tactics Manager Software available from *www.SoccerTutor.com*

Note: While every effort has been made to ensure the technical accuracy of the content of this book, neither the author nor publishers can accept any responsibility for any injury or loss sustained as a result of the use of this material.

Soccer Italian Style Coaches

Mirko Mazzantini
ACF Fiorentina
Academy Coach

Mirko Mazzantini coached at Empoli FC for 10 years, working with all the main age groups at academy level. In 2010 he was recruited by AFC Fiorentina to work with the U14/U15 Academy teams.

During the 2010/11 season Mirko won the U15 Italian Academy Serie 'A' championship.

In 2011/12 Mirko was the Assistant of the Fiorentina Reserve team during pre-season and he was the coach of the ACF Fiorentina U14 team who won the Academy Serie 'A' championship and some international tournaments.

Mirko is currently the ACF Fiorentina U15 coach for the 2012/13 season.

He is a qualified football coach through the "Young Players Coach" program and a UEFA 'B' Licenced Coach, as well as an author of many coaching publications, articles, books and DVDs.

Simone Bombardieri
Empoli FC
Academy Coach

Simone Bombardieri played for Empoli FC for 5 years. He then started his career as a coach for the club 15 years ago at the age of 22, where he has been coaching various academy age groups from U9-U14.

In the 2011/12 season, Simone was the coach of the Empoli FC U14 team who reached the final of the Nick Cup International Tournament, where they lost in extra time against Inter Milan. They also finished eighth in the Academy Serie 'A' championship.

Simone is currently the Empoli FC U15 coach for the 2012/13 season.

He is also a qualified football coach through the "Young Players Coach" program and a UEFA 'B' Licenced Coach, as well as an author of many coaching publications, articles, books and DVDs.

Soccer Italian Style

SOCCER ITALIAN STYLE IS WORLDWIDE...WORK WITH US!

SOCCER ITALIAN STYLE has organised youth football events in many countries around the world. If you are a Club Executive, a Coach, a Technical Director or just an individual passionate about the sport and you want your players to have a unique experience, please contact us or visit our website: www.SoccerItalianStyle.it

PROFESSIONAL ITALIAN CAMP is a week of football for boys and girls aged 6 to 18 years old. It is where fun meets the training methodologies of the best Italian academies and is taught by experienced staff who have worked with with some of highest level clubs in Italy.

PROFESSIONAL ITALIAN TEAM CAMP is a weekly team training camp with the work planned around a highly professional methodology which is tested continuously, innovated and adapted based on the level and characteristics of the participating team.

SOCCER ITALIAN STYLE COACHING CLINICS are organised for all different levels and are based on a proven model that creates lots of interest and enjoyment for the participants. The time spent in the classroom is filled with numerous videos from professional training sessions in Italy and it is supported by on-field demonstrations of the concepts discussed.

NEW INITIATIVE: SOCCER AND TOURISM IN ITALY: Soccer Italian Style has a partnership with an important travel agency to provide a unique experience: improve as a player and sightsee the best parts of Tuscany. Firenze, Pisa, Lucca, Siena, and 5 Terre are just some of the magnificent places waiting for you.

If you want your team to have a week of highly professional training and at the same time be immersed in the culture of Italy, Soccer Italian Style can plan your trip in detail, adapting the itinerary and lodging based on the wishes and needs of the players and chaperones.

The Italian Style Story

Soccer Italian Style was founded in 2005 by 2 passionate professional coaches, Mirko Mazzantini and Simone Bombardieri. Since their first trip overseas, the young coaches' goal has been to share their experiences with passion and professionalism.

The Soccer Italian Style network has spread quickly to many continents through various partnerships, working with youth football clubs, youth football associations and businesses that distribute sports books and videos.

In 2011 Mirko Mazzantini and Simone Bombarideri had the honour to present a lesson at the Coverciano Coaches Training Centre organised by the Italian Football Federation.

Mirko and Simone have received recognition from many countries, and this is reflected in themany contacts and collaborations they have established and by the success of the products developed. This has led to Mirko and Simone visiting many countries throughout the world to share their expertise, particularly in the USA, Canada, Norway, Japan, Australia, New Zealand and many Asian countries. The success enjoyed by Soccer Italian Style has encouraged the founders to increase their efforts with new developments to complement the existing products.

All the initiatives focus on the common denominator; the working philosophy of Soccer Italian Style, as well as the result of personal experiences in professional football clubs, trips around the world and personal experiences.

Numerous coaches, club directors and football fans continuously contact the staff through the website:

www.SoccerItalianStyle.it

As a result of this interest, Mirko and Simone have welcomed other professional coaches and athletic trainers to their football family to help meet the needs of all that are interested.

Contents

CHAPTER 1 10

Introduction 11
1. The Child 12
2. Fundamental Technical Abilities 13
3. Ball Control 14
4. Technical Objectives for U5-8s 15
5. Tactical Objectives: Feints/Dribbling 16
6. Motor Skills 17
7. Coordination 19

CHAPTER 2 20

'Italian Style' Working Methodology - How to Build Your Training Sessions 21
1. The Initial Phase 22
2. The Central Phase 24
3. The Final Phase 25

CHAPTER 3 26

Practice Format 27
The Technical Block 28
The Individual Tactics Block 32

CHAPTER 4 37

SESSION 1 38

1. Warm Up - 'Snow Ball Fight' 38
2. The Technical Block 38
3. Technical Ball Control - 'Downhill Skiing 39
4. Ball Control & Coordination - 'Run in the Trees' 40
5. 2v2 - Free Small Sided Game 41

SESSION 2 42

1. Dribbling Warm Up - 'The Zoo' 42
2. The Technical Block 42
3. Technical - Ball Control & Shooting with 4 Goals 43
4. Technical Dribbling Circuit - 'Grand Prix' 44
5. 1v1 Zones in a 2v2 Small Sided Game 45

SESSION 3 46

1. Ball Control Warm Up - 'Let's Build Together' 46
2. The Technical Block 47

3. Dribble & Collect Game - 'The Supermarket' 47
4. Jump, Dribble and Shoot - 'Who's the Fastest?' 48
5. 2v2 with 4 'Dribble Gates' in a Small Sided Game 49

SESSION 4 50
1. Running with the Ball Warm Up - 'Everybody Out 50
2. The Technical Block 50
3. Dribble, Turn & Shoot - 'The 1v1 Duel' 51
4. Dribbling Duels Game - 'Pirates and Guards' 52
5. 2v2 with 1 End Zone & 1 Goal in a Small Sided Game 53

SESSION 5 54
1. Technical Dribbling Warm Up - 'Traffic Lights' 54
2. The Technical Block 54
3. Ball Control & Awareness Grid -'Dangerous Intersections' 55
4. Dribbling Relay - 'The Metro' 56
5. 2v2 with 4 Goals: 10 Ball Competition in a SSG 57

CHAPTER 5 58
SESSION 6 59
1. Close Ball Control with Shapes - 'The Painters' 59
2. The Technical Block 59
3. 4v4 Dribbling Game - 'The Ball Thief' 60
4. Dribble, Shoot, Roll and Save 61
5. 3v3 - Free Small Sided Game 62

SESSION 7 63
1. Warm Up - 'Hand Ball' 63
2. The Technical Block 64
3. Jump, Dribble & Shoot - 'Let's Work Together' 64
4. Dribble & Tag Game - 'The Rabbit and the Hunter' 65
5. 2v1 Zones in a 3v3 Small Sided Game 66

SESSION 8 67
1. Quick Reactions - 'Odd One Out' Dribbling Game 67
2. The Technical Block 67
3. RWTB in Channels & Shooting - 'The Canoe' 68
4. RWTB in Channels & Shooting -'The Canoe Obstacle Course' 69
5. 1v1 Zones in a 3v3 Small Sided Game 70

SESSION 9 71
1. Aerobic Warm Up - 'Learn the Human Body' 71
2. The Technical Block 71
3. Dribble & Shoot Game - 'Who Score's First?' 72
4. 4v4 Ring Toss Game 73
5. 2v2 (+2) Small Sided Game 74

SESSION 10 75
1. Ball Control Warm Up - 'Walk in the Forest' 75
2. The Technical Block 75
3. Dribbling in an Oval Track - 'Forest Fruits Game' 76
4. Shooting Accuracy Game - 'Catch the Rabbits' 77
5. 2v2 (+2) with 2 Side Zones in a Small Sided Game 78

CHAPTER 6 79

SESSION 11 80
1. Dribbling Warm Up - 'Learn the Names' 80
2. Individual Tactics Block 80
3. 1v1 Duels - 'The Guardian' 81
4. Shooting Practice - '10 Pin Bowling' 82
5. 4v4 with 'End Zones' in a Small Sided Game 83

SESSION 12 84
1. Warm Up - 'Moving Basket Game' 84
2.   Individual Tactics Block 84
3. 1v1 Duels with Gates - 'The Chase' 85
4. Shooting Target Practice - 'The Hole' 86
5. 4v4 with 4 Goals in a Small Sided Game 87

SESSION 13 88
1. Motor Aerobic Warm Up - 'Fantasy Track' 88
2. Individual Tactics Block 88
3. 1v1 Duels Team Game - 'Capture the Flag' 89
4. Speed Ring Relay Game - 'Reach the Finish Line' 90
5. 4v4 with 6 Goals in a Small Sided Game 91

SESSION 14 92
1. 1v1 Warm Up - 'The Battle' 92
2. Individual Tactics Block 92
3. Technical Feints / Moves to Beat - 'The Tunnel' 93
4. Jump, Dribble and Shoot - 'The Tracks' 94
5. 4v4 with 4 Goals in a Small Sided Game 95

SESSION 15 96
1. 6v2 Dribble and Tag Game - 'The Fisherman' 96
2. Individual Tactics Block 96
3. 1v1 Duels Team Game - 'The Net' 97
4. Motor Aerobic Dribbling Game - 'The Dolphin' 98
5. 4v4 with 4 Dribble Gates in a Small Sided Game 99

CHAPTER 7 100

SESSION 16 101
1. Quick Reactions Dribbling Race - 'The Colours'......................................101
2. Individual Tactics Block...101
3. Dribble, Jump and Shoot with Goalkeepers...102
4. Run, Jump and Score First with 4 Players 103
5. 4x4 - Free Small Side Game..104

SESSION 17 105
1. Coordination Circuit Training - 'The Numbers'.....................................105
2. Individual Tactics Block...105
3. 1v1 Back to Goal Duel - 'Turn and Go'...106
4. Football Tennis Game 107
5. 2v2 Zones in a 4v4 Small Sided Game 108

SESSION 18 109
1. Ball Control Warm Up - 'The Alphabet'..109
2. Individual Tactics Block...109
3. 1v1 Duel with a Goal - 'Lateral Defender' 110
4. Throw, Catch, Run, Jump, Dribble and Shoot..111
5. 2v2 Vertical Zones in a 4v4 Small Sided Game 112

SESSION 19 113
1. Running & Dribbling Warm Up - 'Return Home'.......................................113
2. Individual Tactics Block...113
3. 1v1 Frontal Duel with 3 Goals...114
4. Dribbling Multiple Balls / Objects - 'The Move' 115
5. 4v4 with 'Scoring Zones' in a Small Sided Game....................................116

SESSION 20 117
1. Turning and Shooting Game - 'World Cup Qualifiers' 117
2. Individual Tactics Block...117
3. Dribble and Shoot - 'Shooting Range'..118
4. Jump, Dribble and Shoot - 'Shooting Range (2)' 119
5. 4v4 with 6 Dribble Gates in a Small Sided Game 120

CHAPTER

1

Introduction 11

1. The Child 12

2. Fundamental Technical Abilities 13

3. Ball Control 14

4. Technical Objectives for U5-8s 15

5. Tactical Objectives: Feints/Dribbling 16

6. Motor Skills 17

7. Coordination 19

Introduction

This project focuses on the youngest players as it is our main belief that the younger the players are, the more effective the work can be, producing the most visible results.

In the real world, this concept is not shared by everybody and often this delicate age group is treated with superficiality and carelessness.

Very often these young players are assigned to the youngest or to the most inexperienced coaches who are just starting out in their careers. The consequence is that the results achieved are not as expected and the potential of the young players is often not reached.

From our trips across Europe and North America, from sharing ideas with qualified coaches in other countries and from observing other methodologies, we have strengthened our beliefs that have contributed to develop our own methodology which we are about to share with all our readers.

This book is divided into 2 parts which are connected to each other. The first part is the theory where we identify the main concepts of our beliefs, including a brief introduction of the general characteristics of children aged 4 to 8 years old, the technical/tactical and motor objectives and the presentation of the theory model.

The second part is more hands on where we present 20 full sessions with proper progressions, where all the concepts indicated in the first part are easily identified.

We think of the second part as a tool to fully comprehend the concepts explained in the first part of this book. Our hope is that the coaches appreciate and understand our model and that this book is not just used as a source of single and isolated drills.

This book is not meant to be a simple collection of drills and lesson plans, but it is meant to be the presentation of a **new work methodology** which we hope is appreciated and implemented by many coaches and instructors.

The effort put into the completion of this book is a testimonial of our infinite passion for the game of football. We are aware that every day we can learn new things and methodologies and we are very proud to be given the opportunity to share our experience and knowledge.

We thank the editor that has allowed us to produce this book and all the football clubs that have given us the opportunity to work with players of this age.

Mirko Mazzantini and Simone Bombardieri

1. The Child

Every coach working with young players must be aware not only of the technical and tactical concepts, but also of the physical and psychological characteristics of the child during the various periods of growth.

The principal requirement of youth training is adapting the methods of training to the needs of the formation and development of the child.

A training session will be more effective if the coach has accurately studied the methods and how to implement them.

We need to take into consideration that when we work with young children, they are not "miniature adults" so the planning of training sessions for the young players must have a different structure and characteristics from those for the older players.

It is important to know the capabilities and characteristics of a child between the ages of 5 and 8:

1. They have a short attention span and are not able to listen to complex and long explanations.

2. They have difficulty understanding abstract concepts but are able to grasp and imitate an action that is demonstrated.

3. They are still in the stage of "intellectualegocentrism" where they do not yet understand the point of view of other individuals to be different to their own.

4. The child only thinks from their own point of view and they think that everyone else thinks like him, or that everyone else understands their thoughts.

5. They are at a stage where they have full dynamic mental representation of their body. They are conscious of their gestures and movements and for this they are able to mentally control their body in motion. When they picture these images in their heads, their movements become more coordinated and refined.

6. They are dependant on adults and therefore their group of friends is still not too relevant and the coach is predominantly the central figure.

7. From a physical point of view the child is quite frail with little muscle power, however their motor behaviour is still very active.

8. They do not have much control of quick movements. Young children have good joint mobility but their cardiovascular, circulatory and respiratory functions are not yet developed.

9. It is important to know the characteristics of the psychological and physical development of the child to allow the coach to organise and design a plan of work where its content is based largely on fun and practical games.

2. Fundamental Technical Abilities

Football technique covers all the forms of contact allowed by the rules of football. They are called technical abilities and they form the skills with which a player expresses his or her competence. The more the player has confidence with these abilities the more impact they will have in the game.

There are 7 Fundamental Technical Abilities:

1. Running with the ball is the technical gesture that allows the player to move around the pitch. The difficulty is greater as the speed increases, with the presence of opponents and with a reduction of space.

This fundamental technique is often combined with other abilities, like kicking the ball (passing or shooting) and receiving the ball. As far as the age level of this book, this will be mainly associated with kicking the ball to shoot at goal.

2. Kicking the ball, as explained above is intended to teach players to pass if we want to transfer the ball to a teammate, or shoot if the objective is scoring a goal.

3. Receiving the ball is the ability that allows the player to get possession of the ball. When receiving the ball, communication between 2 teammates is completed, but receiving the ball can also occur when intercepting an opponent's pass.

4. Heading the ball: The front and the side of the head is mostly used. Heading has various objectives; it can be used to pass the ball to a teammate, to head the ball at goal, to receive the ball, to intercept or to clear the ball away.

Heading can be used in various conditions, such as diving headers, with feet on the ground, jumping, moving forwards, backwards or diagonally.

5. The Throw in is the only opportunity a player has to handle the ball. It is its uniqueness that categorises the act of throwing as a fundamental technique.

6. Tackling is the technical ability with which the player tries to regain possession of the ball. Tackling requires the presence of an opponent over whom the act of tackling is performed.

7. Goalkeeper technique: Even though the goalkeeper is now more like another player, the goalkeeper clearly has a need for separate techniques compared to the other players because of the use of the hands.

A goalkeeper's technique comprises of all the specific components of this position that must be trained separately and in addition to all the other fundamental techniques. This includes catching, diving, footwork, etc.

3. Ball Control

To the fundamental techniques, we like to add an additional ability that is covered in detail in this book:

Ball control: Although ball control is not a real fundamental technique, it is essential in order to learn and master all the other fundamental techniques we have mentioned.

Ball control is the level of mastery with which the player deals with the ball. The player must be able to have full control of the ball and this requires absolute sensitivity in applying the appropriate muscle tension.

We can divide ball control into 2 categories:

1. Ball control when the ball is in the air (juggling).

2. Ball control when the ball is on the ground.

4. Technical Objectives for U5-8s

Many coaches introduce all the fundamental techniques at this youngest age level. Our opinion is a little different. We think at this age it is more important to concentrate on some of the fundamentals, leaving the others for when they are older.

Our philosophy is due to 2 main reasons:

1. We believe the development of some of the technical abilities is not necessary for this age level, e.g. the long pass in the air (the children do not have the strength and the sensitivity required for this skill), receiving the ball and heading the ball. We believe these fundamentals should be trained at the older age levels.

2. If we work on ball control we will create a solid bas to learn the other technical and tactical fundamentals and increase the ability to deal with 1v1 situations.

This project is based on the idea to create a solid technical base which concentrates on:

1. Running with the ball.

2. Ball control when the ball is on the ground.

3. Kicking, intended as shooting on goal.

Every training session will focus on these fundamentals that will be trained in a unique way so that at the end of the annual plan all the players in the squad will have acquired a reasonable level of ability.

The technical module we have illustrated earlier will be designed around running with the ball and ball control.

Kicking the ball will be trained in all the other exercises, exploiting the motivation component. All children like to shoot on goal and scoring goals is maybe one of the most enjoyable parts of the training session for them.

5. Tactical Objectives: Feints/Dribbling

Tactics (both individual or group) is a very difficult concept. It is not possible to think to introduce tactical concepts at this young age level. The main risk is we would waste precious time which can be devoted to developing fundamental technical objectives. Children at this age are not ready physiologically to face these concepts.

However, we believe there is 1 exception. We believe teaching feints and the simple concept of dribbling, both skills classified as principles of individual tactics when in possession of the ball, are essential objectives that can be introduced and included in the annual working plan of the U5-8 age level.

From a teaching point of view, some of the most common feints like the scissor, the cut, the double step, are just a progression of the technical program of running with the ball and ball control we have mentioned earlier.

Our international experience has confirmed that the younger players are very receptive to teaching the simplest feints. Working consistently on these aspects will help to achieve visible and successful results.

At the end of the season, if the work has been carried out with continuity and with the right methodology, it is reasonable to expect every player to easily perform all the feints we have decided to introduce, although some will do so quicker than others.

We will also see that the players will use the feints to beat an opponent without the encouragement of the coach.

In conclusion, we believe that teaching feints and dribbling to the younger ages is extremely important because players are exposed to the simplest form of a tactical situation, which is the 1v1 duel and this is the key situation to win games in modern football.

The tactical module (Individual Tactics Block) is composed of a series of exercises focusing on feints, dribbling and changes of direction.

6. Motor Skills

The structure of movement is composed of base movements that are called basic motor skills. They allow all the functional activities and they constitute the required ability not just to execute the movements, but to also assume posture positions.

Motor skills are dynamic and are identified as walking, running, jumping, catching, throwing, crawling, rolling and climbing.

Postures are static schemes and are identified as flexing, leaning, running in a circle, bending, elevating, extending, rotating, advancing, swinging, and can include global or segmented movements of the body.

At this point it is important to discuss a key point. In modern society, many children spend most of their day in school or at home and in their spare time they are often either in front of a TV or computer, devoting little time to motor exercises. Because of this, the child does not develop specific motor skills or proper body formation. It is important the coach considers this fact when planning their sessions and expose the child to the elements that have not been taken care of.

During all the phases of child formation it is necessary the coach creates the conditions to increase the range of motor skills and postures.

Many of the technical deficiencies are the result of poor coordination, so working on all these motor skill aspects can only increase the technique of the players.

Therefore, we believe that every coach must set up a full year program including technical objectives and motor skills objectives.

We are now going to examine the motor skills that we propose to include inside the training sessions, with the objective to improve and refine the technique. The inclusion of the activities will also result in more involvement from the player and will be more fun.

1. Walking

Walking is the first motor skill the child executes after he or she can stand and it is the most natural expression of the motor behaviour. At the age of 3 to 5 years old the child already masters this skill which constitutes the base of the first motor experiences.

2. Running

The style of running of a 5 or 6 year old is characterised by lateral swerving, which is not very harmonic and is not efficient. The strides are not regular, but are frequent and short. A child of 9-10 years old who is normally developed can refine this motor skill because his or her coordination capacities and conditional abilities improve.

3. Rolling/Crawling

These skills are found early in children and they constitute one of the first tools to move before they acquire an upright position.

During the school years this skill is not used much and rolling is frequently the source of fear and apprehension. However, they generate fun and enjoyment when used in training sessions.

4. Jumping

The acquisition of this skill requires a certain level of dynamic coordination and control. For a 7-8 year old child the movements of the arms and legs are not well coordinated, especially when in the air. It is essential that in the beginning, jumping low is introduced as a game before progressing to jumping high or long.

5. Catching – Throwing – Kicking

Catching and throwing are motor skills that get developed when increasing the general coordination process, directly related to the relationship between the vision and touch (**Hand-Eye Coordination**).

Only at around 8 years old does throwing become a refined coordinated skill. Catching and kicking depend on the adjustment of the body in the space.

6. Climbing

Like rolling and crawling, climbing is a motor skill that precedes the act of walking. If used during the growth of the child, the skill can be a tool to improve confidence levels and to improve the sense of courage and sense of challenge.

Acquiring the technique of climbing represents a discovery and personal achievement for the child.

Movement, like any other function, develops in a continuous relationship with the environment and through behaviours modified by experience.

The learning of movements goes through the mechanism of perception, coordination, selection and execution that are present in every intentional motor act.

The task of the coach is to promote the progressive control of motor behaviour, taking into consideration what stage the individual is in their bio-physical maturing process.

The different characteristics of development and maturing of the student in a primary school require diversified timing and a method of planning and implementation of motor activity.

During the ages of 3 to 5 and particularly between 5 and 7, the child must develop the capacity of perception, analysis and selection of information that comes from the organising organs.

7. Coordination

In relation to the regulation of movement, an additional series of objectives are represented by the promotion of the coordination capacities that are devoted to the choice of movement, to its direction and its control.

These capacities that are developed intensely between the ages of 6 and 11 are:

Perception, knowledge and awareness of the body

Through the experiences of exploring, discovering, touching, examining, using various parts of the body, playing and manipulating objects, we work on the gradual development of the body in its various aspects. There is an integration of the relationship of emotional, motivational and affective aspects for a complete awareness of the body.

In the football activities presented in this book there are exercises of contact and control of the medium (the ball) to execute with the hands, the feet and with various body parts which allow the child to know and better perceive their own body, acquiring awareness and confidence with the ball. This gives gratification to the child and reiterates their capacities and knowledge.

Hand-Eye Coordination

Particular attention must be given to acquiring this capacity through simple manipulative activities with small objects. This benefits the regularity, precision and the flow of fine motor gestures and graphic learning.

It will be appropriate to introduce activities where the child executes throws, passes and control with the hands. All these activities will benefit general coordination and as a result technique.

Space and time organisation

Using games for exploring the environment will promote the progressive formation and organisation of the physical, geometrical and relational space, and the initial perception of the sequence of the activities.

Using games of movement with predetermined or free structure, with or without objects, in groups or individually, we favour the learning of concepts related to space and orientation (close-far, over-under) and of concepts related to time and to rhythm structures (before, after, slow, fast).

CHAPTER

2

'Italian Style' Working Methodology - How to Build Your Training Sessions............ 21
1. The Initial Phase 22
2. The Central Phase 24
3. The Final Phase 25

'Italian Style' Working Methodology - How to Build Your Training Sessions

As mentioned in the introduction, this book is not meant to be a list of training sessions but an attempt to share our methodology, which can be very rewarding when applied to this particular age level.

The "Italian style" methodology of training represents the structure on which all the training sessions will be based.

All the sessions will follow the same logical structure and are composed of 3 phases:

1) Initial phase

2) Central phase

3) Final phase

Timing	Phase	Description
10 minutes	Initial Phase	Initial Game
15 minutes		Working Block (Technical and Tactical)
10 minutes	Central Phase	Technical Game
15 minutes		Motor Game
10 minutes	Final Phase	Final Game

1. The Initial Phase

The Initial Phase is about 25 minutes long and it is divided into 2 parts:

1. The Initial Game

This initial part of training has a fundamental importance in order to reach our objectives. The Initial Game is where the players are allowed to play in free or themed exercises of running with the ball or control combined with various activities involving motor skills.

The initial exercise must also contain a fun element. This will create a positive mindset in the players which will allow you to get the most out of them in the activities to follow.

This is a delicate phase because the children arrive at training after a long day at school. School commitments and other activities impair the natural impulse of children to free up all their energy and this is visible when they arrive to train.

The children run, scream and chase after each other. All this is used to unleash their enthusiasm and energy. There is no need for additional structure in this phase. We can define this phase as a **warm up** where the children get ready for the second part of the phase.

2. The Working Block

After the initial game, the children will have better focus and concentration and will be more susceptible to learning. This is the time for a type of activity which requires more concentration: **The Working Block**.

The working block is the base of our philosophy. In the other parts of the sessions the coach will create and propose new and fun activities in order to stimulate creativity and avoid repetitive exercises.

Inside the working module we have decided to collect a series of standard exercises which are carefully selected from our experiences on the training pitch that must be repeated during every training session.

These continuous repetitions will allow the players to master the simple but fundamental movements that will form the base for their technical level in the future.

There are 2 different types of working blocks:

1. Technical Working Block

The first module to be used as our working block is the technical block, and as previously mentioned in the technical and tactical objectives section we will focus exclusively on improving the 2 fundamentals:

1. *Running with the ball.*

2. *Ball control.*

We demonstrate all the motor actions that allow the player to run with the ball.These include keeping it under control, changing direction and being able to stop the ball and re-start using as many parts of the foot as possible (the instep, the outside, the sole, the inside etc).

Individual Tactics Working Block

The second module, closely related to the first one, is the individual tactics block. It is important to clarify what we mean by the term tactical in order to avoid any misunderstanding.

In this block we introduce a series of simple exercises, repeated more times uring the course of the season, with the objective to teach simple feints to beat an opponent.

We define the tactical module as such because feints are considered part of individual tactics and because we start introducing the young players

to the tactical objective of beating opponents while maintaining control and possession of the ball.

The exercises contained in the 2 blocks will be shown in detail before the 20 sessions.

Another concept to emphasise is the role of the coach during the course of the technical and tactical blocks. This is the only time during the session where the coach will correct the technical execution of the moves.

The coach will stop the exercise to demonstrate the correct execution, which is a very important moment because the young players learn by imitating a role model.

It is obvious we want to avoid long stops during this moment, so the coach must correct and demonstrate in the least amount of time possible, leaving more time for the players to practice recreating the move.

2. The Central Phase

The Central Phase is characterised by 2 exercises:

1. Technical Game
2. Motor Game

The main difference compared with the previous phase is that during these exercises the coach will not stop the players to correct mistakes of a technical or motor skill nature. The coach will observe and correct without stopping the exercise. This allows the players to repeat the exercise as many times as possible. Sometimes the exercises will require the players to find technical and motor skill solutions without the support of the coach.

From a technical point of view, we introduce the technical skill of kicking the ball, intended mainly as shooting on goal and not as much for passing. Most of the exercises in this phase will end with a shot on goal. This has a double effect, first allowing the player to gain more confidence with this fundamental, and then because the goal represents the ultimate objective for a player it gives the maximum gratification and helps with the flow of a good and fun practice.

The motor exercises will touch on all the motor skills that we described in the technical and tactical objectives section of this book. It will be important to design a general working plan in order to allow the young athletes to consolidate all the motor skills. This will allow for a diverse and complete motor skill development. This type of plan will benefit the technique because if we work

at improving the general coordination of the player, the fundamental technique will improve as well.

Football is a sport where there are no continuous or repetitive movements. The player is required to find solutions to complex situations in the shortest time possible. It is important to work with the youngest players on the physical capacity of quickness. Many times the terms of quickness and speed are confused and to understand the difference think of quickness as the execution of a movement, while speed is the movement inside a space.

This brief explanation is helpful to introduce another important concept when planning a training session. This is with the development of basic motor skills which are important to combine a type of work that includes quickness. The relevance of this objective derives from the fact that although quickness can be improved only in the range between 15% and 20% of thepotential of an athlete, it is at this young age that we can obtain the best results. In an era where football is played in tighter spaces, a slower player will find it more difficult compared to another player with similar skills but with more quickness.

An important element of this phase is that the exercises will be in the form of games with conditions (relay competition etc). As you can imagine, these types of activities stimulate the competition among the players with the benefit of motivation and intensity of training.

3. The Final Phase

The final phase is devoted to the game. It is a very important tool for the coach where he or she can verify the improvements of the squad.

Many coaches also like to see how the players act under a situation of group organisation, asking the players to pass the ball.

Our preference is totally opposite as it is not based on the immediate result, but on trying to stimulate, even in this phase, all the skills that we have worked on during the session.

We will ask the players to execute personal plays through dribbling, running with the ball, ball control and feints, objectives that the players have been working on throughout the session.

In our opinion, with this attitude to the game we can stimulate and work on some aspects of personality and character of the individual, like gaining confidence to try and execute an individual play with creativity and without fear, elements that nowadays are more rare in players.

It is also important to plan a progression starting from simple situations, like 2v2, progressing to a more complex situation like 5v5.

We do not agree with playing games at this age with larger numbers of players on the pitch because the more players we add, the less touches on the ball the players will have.

If there are players that are more advanced in the group compared to others, that factor is amplified with a negative effect on the less developed players.

CHAPTER 3

Practice Format 27
The Technical Block 28
The Individual Tactics Block 32

Practice Format

Each practice in the sessions includes clear diagrams with supporting training notes:

- Name of Practice
- Objective of Practice
- Description
- Variations/Progressions (if applicable)
- Coaching Points

Key

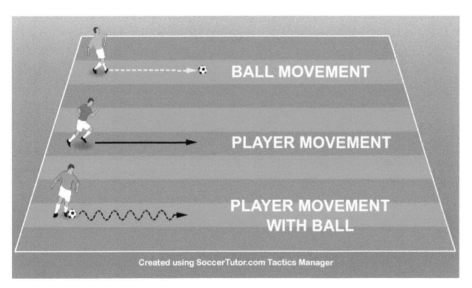

BALL MOVEMENT

PLAYER MOVEMENT

PLAYER MOVEMENT WITH BALL

Created using SoccerTutor.com Tactics Manager

The Technical Block

15 mins

The Technical Block is used for 15 minutes in each of the first 10 sessions and forms the foundation of the player's technique. The players learn how to control/master the ball using all different parts of the feet.

All exercises are played inside this field which is 12 yards x 8 yards (each grid).

The players run with the ball inside the channels in groups of 2-4. All the players use the dribbling technique pre-determined by the coach and dribble from one end to the other and back again.

This technical block has 10 different techniques for running with the ball to practice.

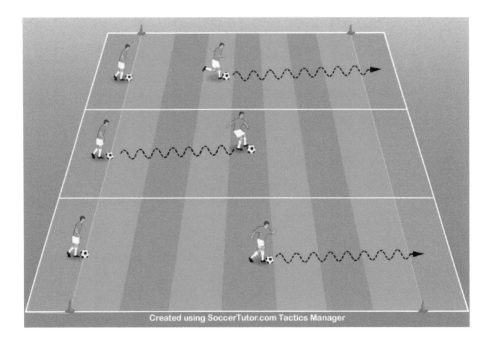

Created using SoccerTutor.com Tactics Manager

Exercise 1 - Move Forward with the Sole

While walking, they push the ball forward using the sole of the right and left foot. The objective is to stimulate ball control and sensitivity. Ask for a soft touch and a regular rhythm.

Exercise 2 - Move the Ball Forward with the Sole while Skipping

While skipping, the players push the ball forward using the sole of the right and left foot while trying to keep a regular and well coordinated rhythm.

Exercise 3 - Inside Rolling with the Sole

The players progress the exercise by rolling the ball inwards with the sole. From a technical point of view the exercise stimulates the sensitivity of the foot to ball contact aimed at improving control. From a motor skill point of view it stimulates joint mobility.

Exercise 4 - Lateral Rolling while Walking

This is a technical exercise where players move the ball forward remaining in a lateral position which is important to learning ball control, feints and dribbling and is characterised by the use of the sole. The body's lateral position will be useful in shielding the ball during a match.

Exercise 5 - Lateral Rolling while Running

This is an exercise of medium difficulty that requires running with constraint and with greater attention and a sensitivity with the touch of the ball linked to the lateral running. This exercise probably reproduces a more realistic match situation of 1v1 where the quickness of execution is high.

Exercise 6 - Running with the Ball with the Inside of the Foot

The players run with the ball using the inside of both feet with quick touches on the ball. The exercise stimulates the contact of the ball and inside of the foot ball control. Progress the exercise by requesting a higher rhythm and quickness of execution.

Exercise 7 - Quick Dribbling using the Outside of the Foot

In this exercise the players run with the ball pushing it quickly with the outside of the foot. The exercise helps the act of dribbling and changes of direction. Emphasise the extension of the foot with the tip pointing down.

Exercise 8 - Dribbling with the Inside and Outside of the Foot with many Quick Touches

In this exercise the players run with the ball using many touches, alternating a touch with the inside and a touch with the outside of the foot. The primary objective of the exercise is the control of the ball and the first steps of dribbling.

Exercise 9 - Dribbling and Stopping

In this exercise the players run with the ball using many touches, and every 3-4 touches they must stop the ball with the sole of the foot. Knowing how to stop the ball and re-start is a technical objective that is very important at this age and also stimulates coordination and balance.

Exercise 10 - Slalom Dribbling

This exercise is the final objective of the technical block and the level of difficulty is high as it represents the peak of this series of exercises. Players run with the ball using quick touches, alternating a touch with the outside and a touch with the inside of the right foot and then repeat the series with the left foot.

The Individual Tactics Block   15 mins

The Individual Tactics Block is used for 15 minutes in each of the sessions 11-20. The players learn how to dominate 1v1s with different feints/moves to beat which provide a foundation for tactical play.

All exercises are played inside this field which is 12 yards x 8 yards (each grid).

The players run with the ball inside the channels in groups of 2-4. All the players use the dribbling technique pre-determined by the coach and dribble from one end to the other and back again.

This individual tactical block has 10 different dribbling techniques/moves to beat to practice.

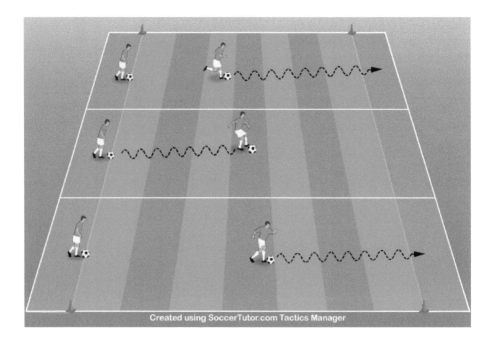

Exercise 1 - Scissor Move

Together the players run forward with the ball and every 2 or 3 touches make a scissor move first with the right foot and then with the left. This is also called a step over.

Exercise 2 - Double Scissor Move

Together the players run forward with the ball and every 2 or 3 touches they make a double scissor move first with the right foot and then with the left. Request a constant foot to ball contact during the exercise and ask for a quick execution of the move. This is also called a double step over.

Exercise 3 - Cut Back Move

Together the players run forward with the ball and every 2 or 3 touches they make a cut back move where the players step over the ball with 1 foot and then cut back with the outside of the same foot. Ask the players to work with both feet. Request a constant foot to ball contact during the exercise and ask for a quick execution of the move.

Exercise 4 - Maradona Move

Together the players run forward with the ball and every 2 or 3 touches they make a Maradona move where the players make a full 360 turn touching the ball with both feet. Request a constant foot to ball contact during the exercise and ask for a quick execution of the move.

Exercise 5 - Chop Move

Together the players run forward with the ball and every 2 or 3 touches they make a Chop move where the player pretends to pass with the inside of the right foot, but instead he plants his foot to the right of the ball and moves in the opposite direction using the outside of the left foot. Do the same with the opposite foot.

Exercises 6-10 utilise a cone or mannequin placed in the middle of the channel. We have groups of 4 and 2 players go at the same time. Start with the players performing their feints/moves to beat to the left of the mannequin and then to the right (avoiding collisions).

When players reach the cone /mannequin they change direction using the specific 'move to beat.'

They are all 'Changes of Direction.'

Request a constant foot to ball contact during the exercise and ask for a quick execution of the move.

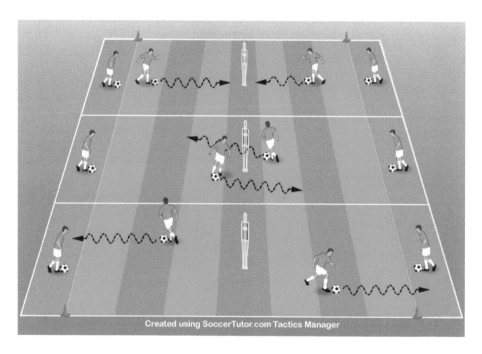

Created using SoccerTutor.com Tactics Manager

Exercise 6 - Sole of the Foot

Players run with the ball until they reach the cone/mannequin, then change direction 180 degrees with the sole of the foot, going back to the starting point.

Exercise 7 - Sole 'L Shape'

Players run with the ball and before the cone/mannequin they change direction pulling the ball first with the sole (step 1) then with the inside of the foot (step 2). When the move is mastered the player will execute the gesture with a single touch of the ball, from sole to the inside of the foot.

Exercise 8 - Inside Of The Foot

Players run with the ball and before the cone/mannequin, they change direction with 1 single touch of the ball with the inside of the foot. A quick execution of the change of direction is needed to sell the move.

Exercise 9 - Outside Of The Foot

Players run with the ball and before the cone/mannequin they change direction with 1 single touch of the ball with the outside of the foot.

Exercise 10 - Internal Cut

Players run with the ball and before the cone/mannequin they change direction by quickly cutting the ball with the inside of the foot (through the legs).

CHAPTER

4

SESSION 1 38

1. Warm Up - 'Snow Ball Fight' 38
2. The Technical Block 38
3. Technical Ball Control - 'Downhill Skiing 39
4. Ball Control & Coordination - 'Run in the Trees' 40
5. 2v2 - Free Small Sided Game 41

SESSION 2 42

1. Dribbling Warm Up - 'The Zoo' 42
2. The Technical Block 42
3. Technical - Ball Control & Shooting with 4 Goals 43
4. Technical Dribbling Circuit - 'Grand Prix' 44
5. 1v1 Zones in a 2v2 Small Sided Game 45

SESSION 3 46

1. Ball Control Warm Up - 'Let's Build Together' 46
2. The Technical Block 47
3. Dribble & Collect Game - 'The Supermarket' 47
4. Jump, Dribble and Shoot - 'Who's the Fastest?' 48
5. 2v2 with 4 'Dribble Gates' in a Small Sided Game 49

SESSION 4 50

1. Running with the Ball Warm Up - 'Everybody Out 50
2. The Technical Block 50
3. Dribble, Turn & Shoot - 'The 1v1 Duel' 51
4. Dribbling Duels Game - 'Pirates and Guards' 52
5. 2v2 with 1 End Zone & 1 Goal in a Small Sided Game 53

SESSION 5 54

1. Technical Dribbling Warm Up - 'Traffic Lights' 54
2. The Technical Block 54
3. Ball Control & Awareness Grid 'Dangerous Intersections' 55
4. Dribbling Relay - 'The Metro' 56
5. 2v2 with 4 Goals: 10 Ball Competition in a SSG 57

SESSION 1

Practice 1

Warm Up - 'Snow Ball Fight'

10 mins

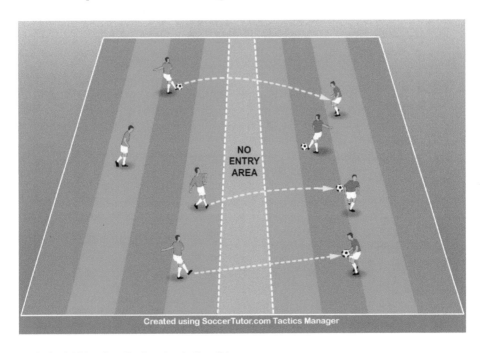

NO
ENTRY
AREA

Created using SoccerTutor.com Tactics Manager

Technical Objective: To develop ball striking accuracy.

Motor Skills Objective: Throw → Catch → Kick.

Description

In a 20 yard x 10 yard area, the players are divided into 2 teams. The field is divided into 3 zones. The players are not allowed in the middle zone which is 2 yards wide. The players will throw/kick the ball and try to hit the players on the other team while trying to dodge the "snow balls" that are being thrown or kicked at them.

Progress from 5 minutes throwing with the hands to 5 minutes kicking the ball with the feet.

Coaching Points

1. Create a positive environment for the training objectives - a 'Mountain Trip'.
2. All the players must participate and execute as many throws/kicks as possible.

Practice 2 - The Technical Block

15 mins

See Pages 28-31

Practice 3

Technical Ball Control - 'Downhill Skiing   10 mins

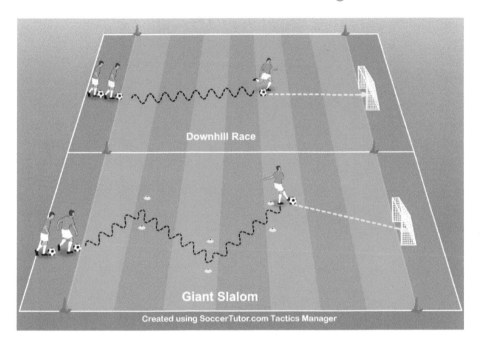

Technical objective: Running with the ball (control/mastery) & striking the ball.

Motor Skills Objective: Running, kicking, coordination, balance and rhythm.

Description
Players are in groups of 2 or 3 and are pretending to ski down a ski slope.

DOWNHILL RACE - (5 mins): For the first 2.5 minutes the players move the ball forward with the sole of both feet and when they are close to the goal they shoot. In the next 2.5 minutes they will run with the ball freely and finish with a shot on goal.

GIANT SLALOM - (5 mins): In this exercises the player will have to make their way through the cone gates before shooting. For the first 2.5 minutes the players move the ball forward with the sole of both feet and will shoot on goal when they are near. For the remaining 2.5 minutes the players will run with the ball freely and will again finish with a shot.

Coaching Points
1. Players should be using small touches, keeping the ball close to their feet.
2. Encourage the children to use both feet in all parts of the exercise.

Practice 4

Ball Control & Coordination - 'Run in the Trees' 15 mins

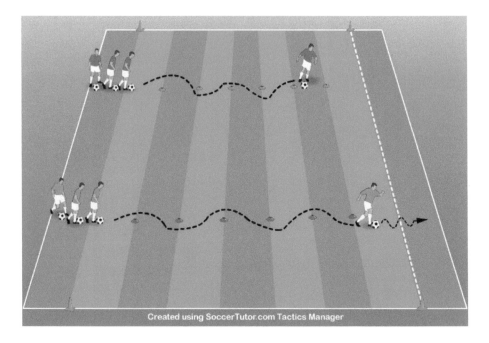

Created using SoccerTutor.com Tactics Manager

Technical objective: To develop the technique for running with the ball (ball control/mastery).

Motor Skills Objective: Running and coordination.

Description
The players run a relay pretending to run between the 'trees' (cones) without touching them.

Variations
1. Run with no ball.
2. Run with the ball in their hands.
3. Dribble the ball with the feet (as shown in diagram).

Coaching Points
1. Change the rhythm of the race by varying the distances between the cones.
2. Encourage competition between the teams to make the exercise more fun.
3. Progress by asking the players to dribble through every second or third cone instead.

Practice 5

2v2 - Free Small Sided Game

10 mins

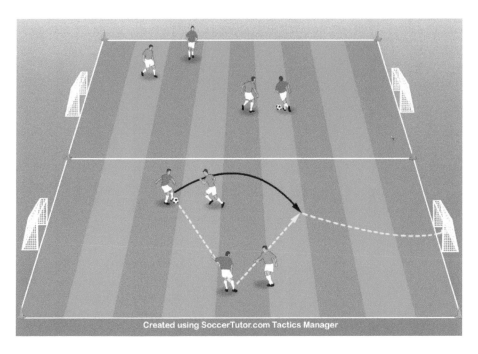

Created using SoccerTutor.com Tactics Manager

Objective
To develop competitive 1v1 play within a team and finishing on goal.

Description
Set up mini-fields where the players play mini games of 2v2.

Coaching Points
1. This is a free game which should stimulate expression, initiative and the creativity of the players.
2. Encourage the players to take each other on and run into space to score.
3. The aim is to develop their technique and individual tactical play.
4. Encourage players to use the dribbling techniques they have learnt in the 'Technical Block.'

SESSION 2
Practice 1
Dribbling Warm Up - 'The Zoo'
10 mins

Created using SoccerTutor.com Tactics Manager

Technical objective: Running with the ball and stopping the ball (ball control/mastery).

Motor Skills Objective: Walk → Run → Jump → Roll → Crawl.

Description
Using an area 8 yards x 12 yards, 8 players dribble the ball freely. The coach calls out an animal and asks the players to use their imagination to imitate the way the animal walks.

Snake: Crawl, Frog: Jump, Cat: Walk on 4 Legs, Lobster: Walk on 4 Legs Backwards.

Coaching Points
1. Teach the children to be aware of each other to avoid collisions.
2. The exercise is fun as the children imitate animals but we also work on their motor skills.
3. Coaches can introduce many more variations.
4. Create a positive environment to stimulate creativity by using role play for the exercise.

Practice 2 - The Technical Block
15 mins
See Pages 28-31

Practice 3

Technical - Ball Control & Shooting with 4 Goals **10 mins**

Created using SoccerTutor.com Tactics Manager

Technical objective: To develop ball control, stopping, turning and shooting accuracy.

Motor Skills Objective: Running, rhythm, balance, coordination and quickness of execution.

Description

Set up a large square 20 yards x 20 yards with a smaller square inside it (10 x 10 yards). Players move with the ball inside the smaller square executing different types of dribbling:

1) Moving the ball forward with the sole of both feet. **2)** Using only the right foot. **3)** Using only the left foot. **4)** Move the ball forward with the instep of both feet. **5)** The coach can introduce a variety of obstacles inside the smaller square (cones, hurdles etc) and the players must dribble the ball trying to avoid them (as shown in diagram).

At the coach's signal all the players must move towards one of the 4 goals and shoot. The last player to score in a goal loses a point. After every 2 signals to shoot at goal, change the type of dribbling.

Coaching Points

1. Players should be learning to use all parts of the foot to dribble.

2. Encourage creativity of the players to use turns and moves.

3. This is a good practice to teach awareness; to avoid the obstacles and other players.

Practice 4

Technical Dribbling Circuit - 'Grand Prix'   **15 mins**

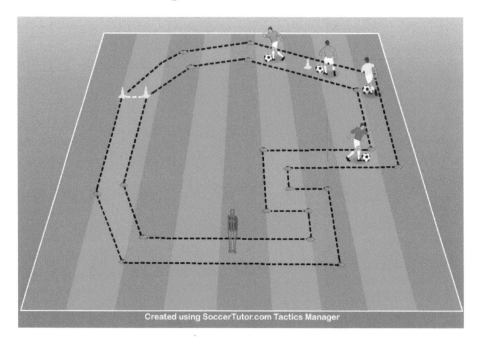

Created using SoccerTutor.com Tactics Manager

Technical objective: To develop ball control, stopping, turning and dribbling in tight areas.

Motor Skills Objective: Running, rhythm, balance, coordination and quickness of execution.

Description

Players are divided into groups of 4 and must dribble the ball inside the race track, pretending to be a race car driver.

First the players race without the ball, then we introduce obstacles on the track to be dodged/jumped and finally the players run with the ball. If a player loses control of the ball and the ball goes out, they can re-enter the track from where they went out.

Coaching Points

1. Players need to use small touches keeping the ball close to their feet.
2. Make sure both feet are used for the entirety of this practice.
3. Heads need to be up to be able to see the obstacles and dribble round them.
4. Create a positive and fun environment stimulating the competition.
5. Stress the importance of increasing the speed in this exercise as it is a race.

Practice 5

1v1 Zones in a 2v2 Small Sided Game

10 mins

Created using SoccerTutor.com Tactics Manager

Objective

To develop competitive 1v1 play with attacking/defending and finishing on goal. There are also elements of passing and receiving with the use of zones.

Description

The pitch is divided into 2 halves. In each half, there is a 1v1 situation and players are not allowed to enter the opposite half. Start the play with the hands (to score: throw the ball in the goal). Then quickly progress to play with the feet. Change the player positions so all get to attack and defend.

Coaching Points

1. This is a free game which should stimulate expression, initiative and the creativity of the players.

2. Encourage the players to take each other on and run into space to score.

3. The aim is to develop their technique and individual tactical play.

4. Encourage players to use the dribbling techniques they have learnt in the 'Technical Block.'

SESSION 3
Practice 1
Ball Control Warm Up - 'Let's Build Together'

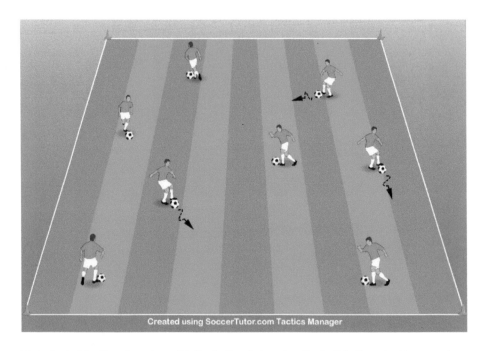

Created using SoccerTutor.com Tactics Manager

Technical objective: Running with the ball and stopping the ball (ball control/mastery).

Motor Skills Objective: Walk → Run → Jump → Roll → Crawl.

Description
In an area 8 yards x 12 yards, 8 players dribble freely in the space. The coach will tell a story where all the players moving with the ball must participate in building something, like a school. Listening out for a call from the coach, the players must execute a technical move with control of the ball. Here are some examples:

LAWN MOWER - The players run freely on the field pretending to cut the grass.
TRACTOR - Players jump on the ball with the sole of the foot pretending to level the ground.
CARPENTER- The players move the ball quickly side to side with the inside of both feet and this builds the walls and rooms of the school.

Coaching Points
1. Players need to use both feet, while also practicing using different parts of the foot.
2. Monitor the different dribbling techniques, with the players using soft touches.
3. Awareness should be taught so heads are up and players avoid any collisions.
4. Make sure the practice is fun with the role play of building something together.

Practice 2 - The Technical Block   15 mins
See Pages 28-31

Practice 3
Dribble & Collect Game - 'The Supermarket'   10 mins

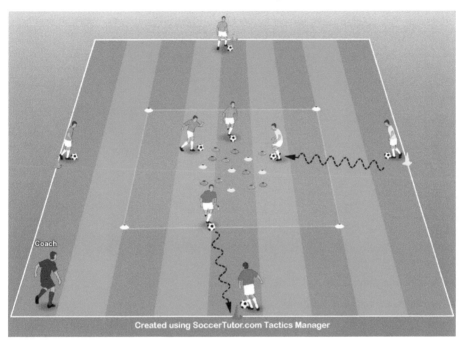

Technical objective: Running with the ball and stopping the ball (ball control/mastery).

Motor Skills Objective: Running, coordination, reactions, orientation and speed of execution.

Description
Set up a large square 20 yards x 20 yards with a smaller square inside it (10 x 10 yards). Inside the smaller square, there are various cones that represent food items. We have 4 teams who all have a home on one of the 4 sides of the larger square (shown with the red, yellow and orange cones).

On the coach's call, 1 player per team will leave their home to fetch a cone of the colour of the food item called by the coach (eg. if the coach calls a tomato, the players will collect the red cones). The players can only collect 1 cone at a time. The team that collects the most cones in a set time period will win the game. Progress from running without the ball to running with the ball.

Coaching Points
1. Players should use the various types of dribbling from the previous practice.
2. Coordination and balance are key as the players need to sprint, stop and turn quickly.

Practice 4

Jump, Dribble and Shoot - 'Who's the Fastest?'   15 mins

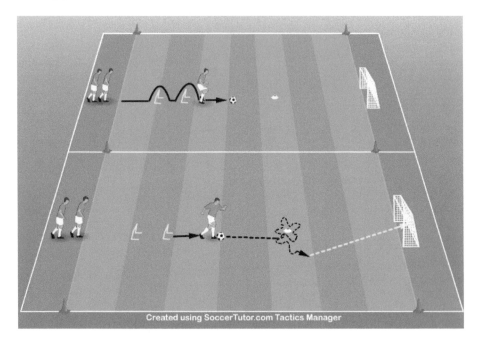

Technical objective: Close ball control and ball striking accuracy.

Motor Skills Objective: Coordination to change from walking to jumping to running. This includes an importance on rhythm and balance.

Description

This practice is a relay between 2 teams. Every player must jump over the low hurdles, run to where the ball is (as shown in diagram) and dribble the ball around the cone, before shooting on goal. Running backwards, the player picks up the ball from the goal and places it on the spot, then runs to his teammate for a high five. The next player goes. The team who score 10 goals first win the game.

Variations: 1) Increase the number of low hurdles. **2)** The player picks up the ball and shoots with a volley for the shot at the end.

Coaching Points

1. Make sure to use hurdles no large than 6 inches for these young players.
2. Soft touches, keeping the ball close to the feet needed for going round the cone.
3. Accuracy is the key for the shot on goal, not the power.
4. Encourage fun and competition, with the players needing to quickly get back to tag their teammates in this race.

Practice 5

2v2 with 4 'Dribble Gates' in a Small Sided Game   **10 mins**

Created using SoccerTutor.com Tactics Manager

Objective

To develop the technique for dribbling and feints/moves to beat in competitive 1v1 play within a team.

Description

We have 2 goals at each end made from traffic cones and poles. To score a goal, players have to dribble the ball through the gate and stop the ball with the sole of the foot beyond the goal.

Coaching Points

1. This is a free game which should stimulate expression, initiative and the creativity of the players.

2. Encourage the players to take each other on and run into space to score.

3. The aim is to develop their technique and individual tactical play.

4. Encourage players to use the dribbling techniques they have learnt in the 'Technical Block.'

SESSION 4
Practice 1
Running with the Ball Warm Up - 'Everybody Out **10 mins**

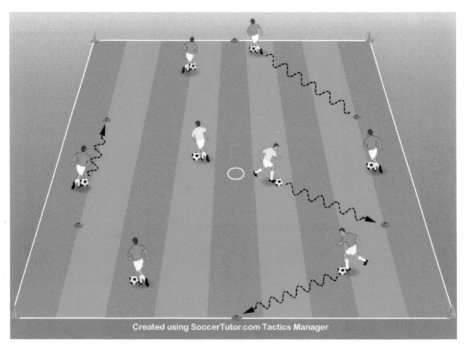

Created using SoccerTutor.com Tactics Manager

Technical objective: Running with the ball and stopping the ball (control/mastery).
Motor Skills Objective: Running, coordination, adapting and orientation.

Description
In an area 15 yards x 15 yards, 8 players are divided as follows: 6 players are inside their own home (standing by a blue cone) and 2 players are in the middle of the field (by the yellow speed ring). On the call of the coach, all the players must leave their home and try to reach another one. The 2 middle players who do not have a home must try and move to occupy one that is available.

The 2 players who are are last to the cones become the middle men and lose a point. Start without the ball and quickly progress to running with the ball. The ball must be stopped on the home (cone) and they are not allowed to go past it.

Coaching Points
1. Players need to be aware of the movement of others to decide where best to run.
2. When dribbling they need to be quick, but make sure good control is maintained

Practice 2 - The Technical Block   **15 mins**
See Pages 28-31

Practice 3

Dribble, Turn & Shoot - 'The 1v1 Duel'

10 mins

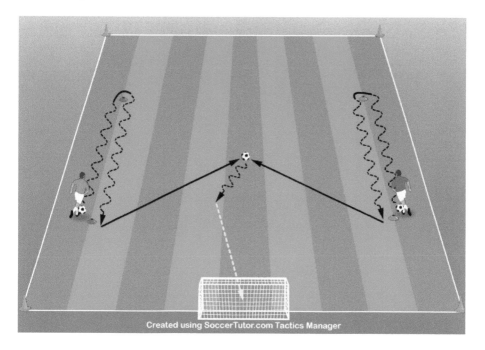

Created using SoccerTutor.com Tactics Manager

Technical objective: Close ball control, 1v1 play and ball striking accuracy (shooting).

Motor Skills Objective: Run, kick, coordination (balance/rhythm) & quickness of execution.

Description

In an area 10 yards x 15 yards, 2 players start from the cone nearest the goal. They dribble round the opposite cone and back to the starting point where they leave their ball. They then run towards the ball in the centre and the first to arrive to the ball becomes the attacker and tires to score in the goal. The player that is second to the ball becomes the goalkeeper.

Variation: You can start the first 5 minutes of the drill with the players carrying the ball in their hands for the first phase around the cones.

Coaching Points

1. Create a positive environment to stimulate the competitiveness and speed.
2. During the dribbling phase, the players should first run quickly with the ball before slowing down, using soft touches to turn around the cone.

Practice 4

Dribbling Duels Game - 'Pirates and Guards'   **15 mins**

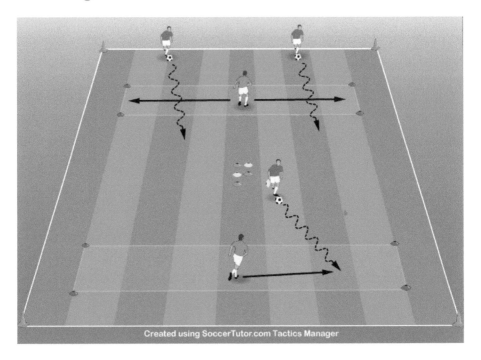

Created using SoccerTutor.com Tactics Manager

Technical objective: Running with the ball, 1v1 play and stopping/starting while dribbling.

Motor Skills Objective: Run, coordination, reactions, orientation & quickness of execution).

Description

In an area 20 yards x 20 yards there are various cones ('Treasure') in the centre of the field. There is 1 guard in each of the 2 corridors as shown in the diagram.

The players with the ball want to dribble through the first corridor, pick up a piece of treasure and then dribble through the second corridor to safety. The first guard must try to prevent the pirates from getting to the treasure and the second guard must prevent the pirates from getting to safety with their stolen treasure (both by trying to win the ball).

Coaching Points

1. Change roles often so players can be the pirates and the guards.
2. Encourage creativity for when the pirates dribble past the guards.

Practice 5

2v2 with 1 End Zone & 1 Goal in a Small Sided Game 10 mins

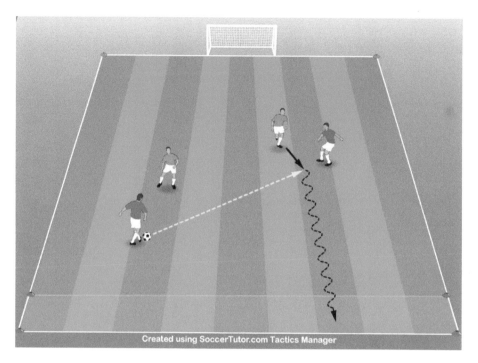

Created using SoccerTutor.com Tactics Manager

Objective
To practice running with the ball and stopping the ball in competitive 1v1 play within a team and ball striking accuracy (shooting).

Description
In this 2v2 game, we have a goal at one end and an 'End Zone' at the other end. One team (blue) aims to score in the goal and the others (red) score by dribbling into the 'End Zone' and stopping the ball with the sole of the foot. 1 point is awarded for stopping the ball in the 'End Zone' and 2 points for scoring in the goal. Change the team roles halfway through.

Coaching Points
1. This is a free game which should stimulate expression, initiative and the creativity of the players.
2. Encourage the players to take each other on and run into space to score.
3. The aim is to develop their technique and individual tactical play.
4. Encourage players to use the dribbling techniques they have learnt in the 'Technical Block.'

SESSION 5
Practice 1
Technical Dribbling Warm Up - 'Traffic Lights' **10 mins**

Created using SoccerTutor.com Tactics Manager

Technical objective: Running with the ball and stopping the ball (ball control/mastery).

Motor Skills Objective: Coordination (reactions, transformation and orientation).

Walk → Run → Stop → Jump → Roll → Crawl.

Description
In an area 8 yards x 12 yards, 8 players run with the ball freely. The coach will hand out bibs with different colours which correspond to various styles of running with the ball:

Red Bibs: Players walk, Yellow Bibs: Players run, Blue Bibs: Players sit on the ball, stop it with the foot and jump or roll, Orange Bibs: Run on 4 legs/Crawl.

Coaching Points
1. The players need to be aware of each other to avoid collisions, especially when jumping, rolling or crawling.
2. This exercise should be fun but the aim is to keep control of the ball at all times.

Practice 2 - The Technical Block **15 mins**
See Pages 28-31

Practice 3

Ball Control & Awareness Grid – 'Dangerous Intersections'

10 mins

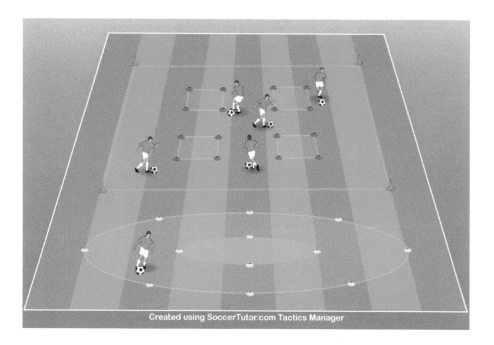

Created using SoccerTutor.com Tactics Manager

Technical objective: Dribbling the ball in tight areas (control/mastery) and awareness.

Motor Skills Objective: Running, rhythm, balance, coordination and orientation.

Description

Players have a ball each and dribble inside 'the street'. Every time they get to the intersection they must avoid all the other drivers, paying attention to the control of their ball and stopping the ball if necessary.

If a player collides with another player, they must go back to driving school (the oval track) to 'learn how to drive' and must complete 2 laps of the circuit before returning to 'the street'.

Variations: 1) Dribble with both feet. **2)** Dribble with only the right foot. **3)** Dribble with only the left foot. **4)** Dribble using the soles of both feet. **5)** Introduce obstacles on the road (hurdles - "other cars" or mannequins - "pedestrians").

Coaching Points

1. Create a fun environment with good role play of pretending to be cars on the road.
2. The correct execution of running with the ball is key with close control, being able to stop the ball when necessary and then quickly start again.

Practice 4
Dribbling Relay - 'The Metro'

15 mins

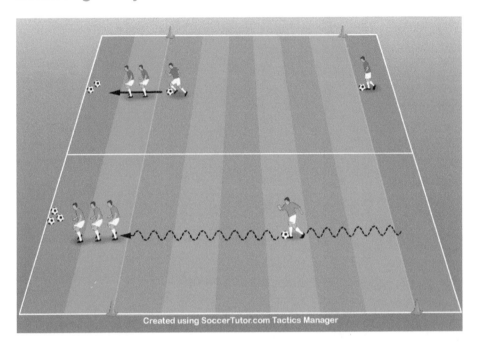

Created using SoccerTutor.com Tactics Manager

Technical objective: Dribbling (ball control/mastery) with an emphasis on speed.

Motor Skills Objective: Run → Stop → Crawl → Jump.

Description
In an area 10 yards x 20 yards, 2 teams compete in a game where the aim is to join 4 carriages of a metro train in a station. The 'carriages' (players) must crawl under all the other carriages (players with open legs) and go to the front. The team that arrives first at the station with all 4 'carriages' wins the game.

Start without the ball and then progress to giving a ball to each player which they must bring the entire way. A variation is to get the players to leap frog over the other players instead of crawling underneath them.

Coaching Points
1. The speed of play is key here as it is a competition.
2. Monitor the rhythm of running fast and then slowing down at the optimum time to then be able to crawl or jump.
3. Players should use both feet and all different parts of the foot when dribbling.

Practice 5

2v2 with 4 Goals: 10 Ball Competition in a SSG   **10 mins**

Created using SoccerTutor.com Tactics Manager

Objective
To develop quick reactions with competitive 1v1 play (within a team) and finishing on goal.

Description
The coach has 10 balls in the corner or outside the area and he passes them 1 at a time into the centre. When a goal is scored or the ball goes out, the coach passes the next ball in.

There are 4 goals and both teams can score in any of them. The team that scores the most goals using these 10 balls wins.

Coaching Points
1. This is a free game which should stimulate expression, initiative and the creativity of the players.
2. Encourage the players to take each other on and run into space to score.
3. The aim is to develop their technique and individual tactical play.
4. Encourage players to use the dribbling techniques they have learnt in the 'Technical Block.'

CHAPTER
5

SESSION 6 59
1. Close Ball Control with Shapes - 'The Painters' 59
2. The Technical Block 59
3. 4v4 Dribbling Game - 'The Ball Thief' 60
4. Dribble, Shoot, Roll and Save 61
5. 3v3 - Free Small Sided Game 62

SESSION 7 63
1. Warm Up - 'Hand Ball' 63
2. The Technical Block 64
3. Jump, Dribble & Shoot - 'Let's Work Together' 64
4. Dribble & Tag Game - 'The Rabbit and the Hunter' 65
5. 2v1 Zones in a 3v3 Small Sided Game 66

SESSION 8 67
1. Quick Reactions - 'Odd One Out' Dribbling Game 67
2. The Technical Block 67
3. RWTB in Channels & Shooting - 'The Canoe' 68
4. RWTB in Channels & Shooting - 'The Canoe Obstacle Course' .69
5. 1v1 Zones in a 3v3 Small Sided Game 70

SESSION 9 71
1. Aerobic Warm Up - 'Learn the Human Body' 71
2. The Technical Block 71
3. Dribble & Shoot Game - 'Who Score's First?' 72
4. 4v4 Ring Toss Game 73
5. 2v2 (+2) Small Sided Game 74

SESSION 10 75
1. Ball Control Warm Up - 'Walk in the Forest' 75
2. The Technical Block 75
3. Dribbling in an Oval Track - 'Forest Fruits Game' 76
4. Shooting Accuracy Game - 'Catch the Rabbits' 77
5. 2v2 (+2) with 2 Side Zones in a Small Sided Game 78

SESSION 6
Practice 1

Close Ball Control with Shapes - 'The Painters'   **10 mins**

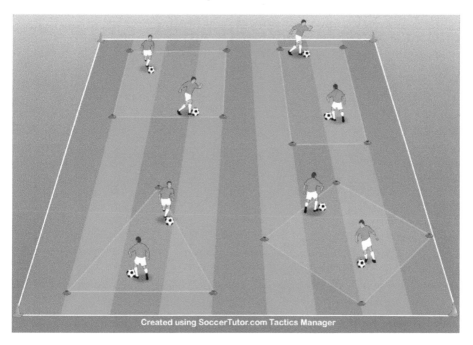

Created using SoccerTutor.com Tactics Manager

Technical objective: Running with the ball and stopping (ball control/mastery).
Motor Skills Objective: Walking, running, coordination and imagery.

Description
In an area 20 yards x 20 yards, cones are placed to represent geometric shapes (square, rectangle, triangle & diamond). The players are in pairs and the coach tells them to draw the various shapes. 1 player imagines the ball is a brush and will paint the outline of the shape, while the other will pretend to paint the inside.

Variation: Form a more complex shape like a house and assign each player a different task, such as paint the walls, the roof, the windows, etc.

Coaching Points
1. Introduce competition between the pairs to speed up the correct execution.
2. Observe and demonstrate the correct method of running with the ball for the 2 different roles.

Practice 2 - The Technical Block   **15 mins**
See Pages 28-31

Practice 3

4v4 Dribbling Game - 'The Ball Thief'   **10 mins**

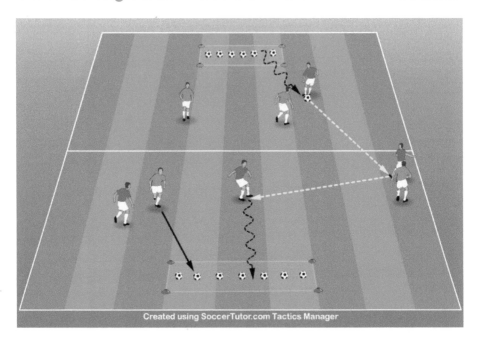

Created using SoccerTutor.com Tactics Manager

Technical objective: Running with the ball and stopping (ball control/mastery).

Motor Skills Objective: Running, coordination, adapting, balance & quickness of execution.

Description
In an area 20 yards x 20 yards, the players are divided into 2 teams and are protecting their zone where the 'safe' is located. inside the safe there are 7 balls. At the coach's command, the players must run inside the opponent's half and steal a ball (1 at a time) from the safe and try to bring it back to their own safe.

The team with the most balls after 8 minutes win. Use the last 2 minutes for each player on the winning team to take a penalty against the losing players who become goalkeepers.

Variations: 1) Use the hands to start. **2)** Progress to dribbling with the ball.

Coaching Points
1. Encourage the players to use 1v1 play to dribble round their opponents, with a focus on speed and creativity.
2. Players should use the sole of their foot to stop the ball in their 'safe.'

Practice 4
Dribble, Shoot, Roll and Save

15 mins

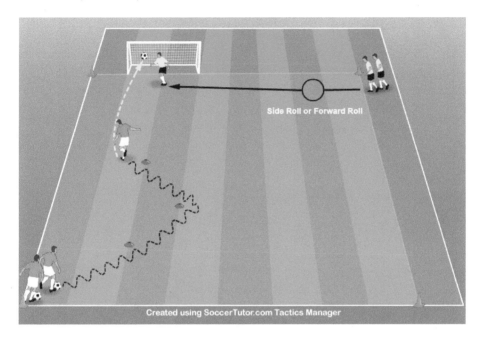

Side Roll or Forward Roll

Created using SoccerTutor.com Tactics Manager

Technical objective: Running with the ball and ball striking accuracy (shooting).

Motor Skills Objective: Run, crawl, roll, coordination, balance & quickness of execution.

Description
In an area 10 yards x 15 yards, we split the players into 2 teams. Both teams start at the same point and go one at a time. One team will run with the ball round and through the cones as shown and then shoot at goal.

The other team are the goalkeepers and after they do a roll as shown in the diagram, they try to save the shot. After each shot the 2 players change positions (they run to the end of the other queue).

Coaching Points
1. Monitor the correct execution of running with the ball round the cones.
2. Players need to keep the ball close to their feet using soft touches.
3. The speed of play should be high for the player and the goalkeeper to get into position.

Practice 5

3v3 - Free Small Sided Game

10 mins

Created using SoccerTutor.com Tactics Manager

Objective
To develop competitive 1v1 play within a team and finishing on goal.

Description
Set up mini-fields where the players play mini games of 3v3.

Coaching Points
1. This is a free game which should stimulate expression, initiative and the creativity of the players.
2. Encourage the players to take each other on and run into space to score.
3. The aim is to develop their technique and individual tactical play.
4. Encourage players to use the dribbling techniques they have learnt in the 'Technical Block.'

SESSION 7
Practice 1
Warm Up - 'Hand Ball'

10 mins

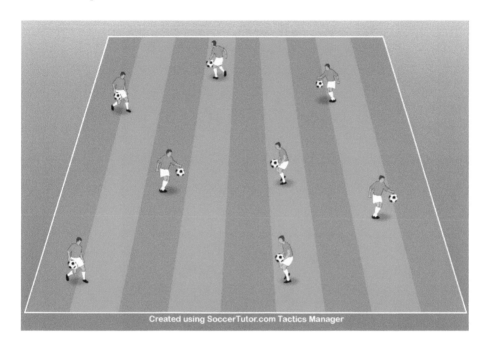

Created using SoccerTutor.com Tactics Manager

Technical objective: Ball to hand contact and control.

Motor Skills Objective: Running, rolling, throwing, catching & hand-eye coordination.

Description
In an area 8 yards x 12 yards, 8 players move around with the ball in their hands. The coach will call out different games. Create a competition using a points system.

1. "Throw the ball in the air and catch it."
2. "Throw the ball in the air, clap the hands (once or twice) and catch it."
3. "Run and bounce the ball like a basketball."
4. "Throw the ball in the air, do a roll (side or forward) and then catch it again."
5. "Find a teammate and throw the ball in the air to each other to swap."
6. "Throw the ball, roll on the ground and catch it after 2 bounces."

Coaching Points
1. Every coach can use their imagination to make the game more fun.
2. Create a positive environment using competition with the points system.
3. Stimulate contact with the ball using various methods of manipulating the ball.

Practice 2 - The Technical Block	15 mins
See Pages 28-31	

Practice 3
Jump, Dribble & Shoot - 'Let's Work Together' 10 mins

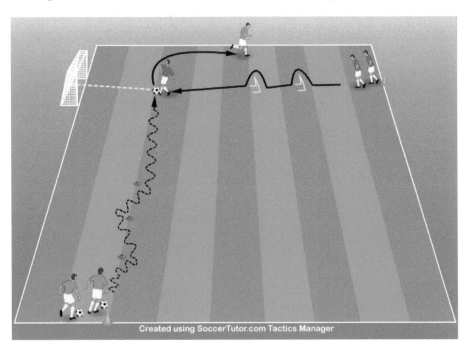

Created using SoccerTutor.com Tactics Manager

Technical objective: Running with the ball, stopping the ball (control) and shooting.

Motor Skills Objective: Run, crawling, jumping, motor combinations, speed and agility.

Description
In an area 10 yards x 20 yards, there are 2 lines of players. One line dribbles the ball around the cones and then stop the ball in front of the goal as shown in the diagram.

The other line of players jump over the hurdles or roll under them and shoot in the goal. The players exchange roles after each shot (join the other queue).

Variations
1. The players dribble with both feet.
2. The players dribble using the sole of both feet.
3. The players pick up the ball and volley the ball after 1 bounce to shoot in the goal.

Coaching Points
1. Observe the ability of ball control and demonstrate the proper execution.
2. Depending on the age of the players and the height of the hurdles, either get the players to crawl under the hurdles or jump over them using your best judgment.

Practice 4

Dribble & Tag Game – 'The Rabbit and the Hunter' 15 mins

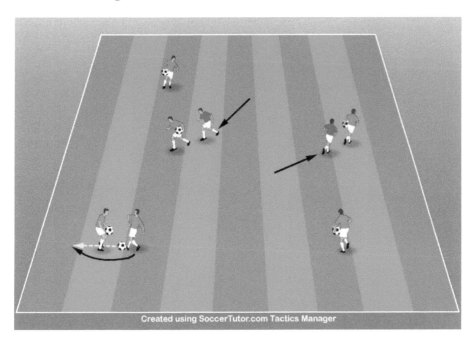

Created using SoccerTutor.com Tactics Manager

Technical objective: Running with the ball, (ball control/mastery).

Motor Skills Objective: Running, crawling and keeping hold of/carrying the ball.

Description
In an area 15 yards x 15 yards, the players move freely in the box. There are 2 hunters and 6 rabbits. The hunters capture the rabbits by tagging them.

Once captured, the rabbits must stop on the spot and open their legs wide. The other rabbits must crawl under the legs of the captured rabbit to give them freedom. Every 1.5 minutes the hunters change.

Variations: 1) Once the rabbits are captured they must crouch down. To get freedom, the other rabbits must jump over them. **2)** All the rabbits have a ball in their hands and to get freedom the ball must be passed under their legs and picked up on the other side (Diagram).

Coaching Points
1. Reinforce the need for full concentration and awareness to avoid any collisions.
2. Urge the players to help their teammates when they are stuck.
3. In the second variation, the pass through the legs should be soft so they can receive the ball again on the other side of their teammate.

Practice 5

2v1 Zones in a 3v3 Small Sided Game

10 mins

Created using SoccerTutor.com Tactics Manager

Objective

To develop competitive 1v1 play with attacking/defending and finishing on goal. There are elements of passing and receiving which are necessary to transfer the ball between zones.

Description

The pitch is divided into 2 halves and we play a 3v3 game. In each half there are 2 attackers and 1 defender, so there is a 2v1 situation on both sides.

A defender starts with the ball and tries to pass to their teammates in the other half to score. The other team's attackers try to win the ball from the defender to score themselves.

Coaching Points

1. This is a free game which should stimulate expression, initiative and the creativity of the players.

2. Encourage the players to take each other on and run into space to score.

3. Change roles often so all players defend and attack during the exercise.

4. Encourage players to use the dribbling techniques they have learnt in the 'Technical Block.'

SESSION 8
Practice 1
Quick Reactions - 'Odd One Out' Dribbling Game **10 mins**

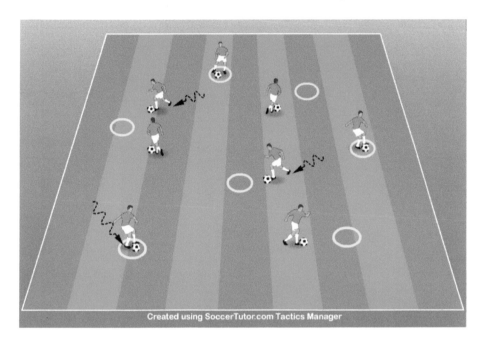

Created using SoccerTutor.com Tactics Manager

Technical objective: Running with the ball, stopping the ball (ball control/mastery).

Motor Skills Objective: Running, jumping and awareness of space and time.

Description

Players run in a square 15 yards x 15 yards. Every player will start with 3 points and dribble freely around the square. At the call of the coach, they must stop inside the rings that are scattered inside the square. The number of rings will be 1 less than the number of players.

The player that does not find a ring will lose a point. The first player to zero will be eliminated and will wait for the end of the game while dribbling the ball outside the square in a pre-set circuit. When someone goes out, remove 1 ring.

Variations: 1) Start without a ball and the player must stop inside the ring, balancing on the right foot or on the left foot, or he must sit, crouch etc. **2)** The players use a ball to play the game. When stopping, the ball and player must be inside the ring.

Practice 2 - The Technical Block   **15 mins**
See Pages 28-31

Practice 3

RWTB in Channels & Shooting - 'The Canoe'   10 mins

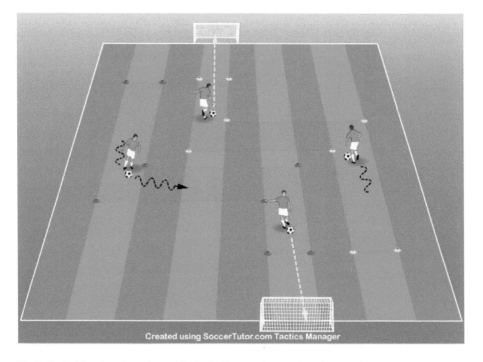

Created using SoccerTutor.com Tactics Manager

Technical objective: Running with the ball, stopping the ball (control) and shooting.

Motor Skills Objective: Running, kicking and quickness of execution.

Description

In an area 20 yards x 20 yards, 2 goals are placed on the pitch connected by 2 'Rivers'. The players must run with the ball inside the river pretending to be in a canoe. Without going outside of the river, they must stop the ball and shoot in the goal.

After the shot, the player picks up the ball out of the goal and starts dribbling the ball along the other river towards the other goal.

Variations: 1) Shooting without stopping the ball. **2)** Set some obstacles to be avoided inside the rivers.

Coaching Points

1. Players need to keep the ball close to their feet, especially around the turns.
2. When shooting, the head should be over the ball and the non-striking foot should be placed next to the ball to maximise accuracy.

Practice 4

RWTB in Channels & Shooting – 'The Canoe Obstacle Course'

15 mins

Side or Forward Roll

Created using SoccerTutor.com Tactics Manager

Technical objective: Ball control/mastery and shooting.

Motor Skills Objective: Run → Crawl → Jump → Roll → Crawl → Kick.

Description

Using the same field as in the previous game we now introduce 3 hurdles in one direction and 2 mats in the other direction.

In the first direction, the players must crawl under the hurdles and shoot in the goal with one of the balls that are placed at the end of the river.

They then return the ball to the shooting spot and join the other 'river' going in the opposite direction. When they reach the first mat they must do a forward roll and on the second mat they roll on their side.

Coaching Points

1. Demonstrate both rolls and help the players to do a forward roll if they need.
2. Monitor the execution of the motor gestures, ie. crawling under the hurdles.
3. For older players, you can get them to jump over low hurdles.

Practice 5
1v1 Zones in a 3v3 Small Sided Game   **10 mins**

Created using SoccerTutor.com Tactics Manager

Objective
To develop competitive 1v1 play and finishing on goal. We also introduce the players to different roles and areas of the pitch (defence, midfield & attack).

Description
Divide the playing area into 3 zones as shown and we play 3v3. In each zone there is a 1v1 situation with each team having 1 defender, 1 midfielder and 1 attacker.

Start with the hands and quickly progress to use the feet. Change the roles of the players often.

Coaching Points
1. This is a free game which should stimulate expression, initiative and the creativity of the players.
2. Encourage the players to take each other on and run into space to score.
3. When they are using their hands, if the ball touches the ground, the other team re-start.
4. Encourage players to use the dribbling techniques they have learnt in the 'Technical Block.'

SESSION 9
Practice 1
Aerobic Warm Up - 'Learn the Human Body'   **10 mins**

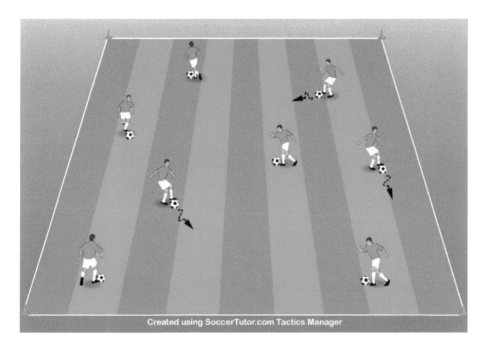

Created using SoccerTutor.com Tactics Manager

Technical objective: Running with the ball and stopping the ball (control/mastery).

Motor Skills Objective: Running and discovering/using different parts of the body.

Description
In an area 8 yards x 12 yards, 8 players dribble the ball freely. The players start with 3 points. The coach will call out a part of the body with which the players will have to stop the ball. The last player to successfully stop the ball loses a point.

Variations: 1) With the hands. **2)** With the knee. **3)** With the head. **4)** With the back.**5)** With the stomach. **6)** Any others from the coach's imagination.

Coaching Points
1. Demonstrate stopping the ball with the various parts of the body.
2. As this is a competition, make sure that all participate fully and respect the rules.

Practice 2 - The Technical Block   **15 mins**
See Pages 28-31

Practice 3

Dribble & Shoot Game - 'Who Score's First?'   10 mins

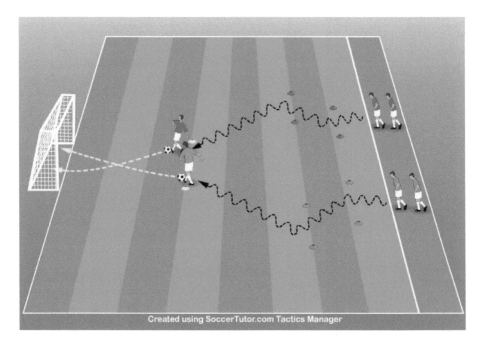

Created using SoccerTutor.com Tactics Manager

Technical objective: Running with the ball and stopping (control/mastery).

Motor Skills Objective: Running, turning, kicking and quickness of execution.

Description
In an area 20 yards x 15 yards, 2 players start with the ball and dribble in between the gates made out of cones. The last gate is common for both players. The player who scores first gets 2 points and the second player gets 1 point if they score.

Variations
1. Players simply run through the gates and shoot one of the 2 balls that are placed after the last gate.
2. Progress to the players running through the gates dribbling the ball and then shooting.

Coaching Points
1. Create a positive environment stimulating competition and quickness of execution.
2. Observe and demonstrate the proper execution of running/dribbling with the ball.

Practice 4
4v4 Ring Toss Game

15 mins

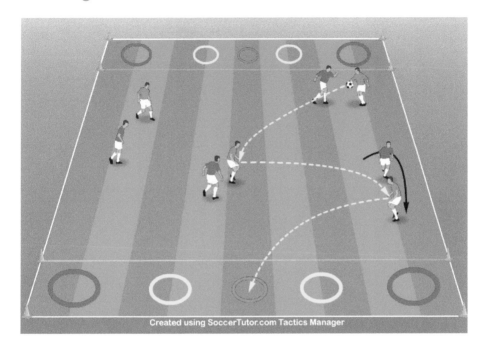

Created using SoccerTutor.com Tactics Manager

Technical objective: Control and contact of the ball with throwing.

Motor Skills Objective: Running, catching and throwing.

Description
In an area 20 yards x 15 yards, 2 teams play a 4v4 game. The aim is for a player to throw the ball into one of the 3 rings that are placed at the end in the outside zones.

Variations
1. Use rings with different colours/sizes and assign different points to the different rings (red ring is 3 points, yellow is 2 points and the blues are 1 point).
2. If you do not have different size rings, just vary the distance away from the playing area.

Coaching Points
1. During this practice the coach needs to encourage the players to work together as a team.
2. Early stages of awareness and running into space are developed during this drill.
3. If you do not have rings, just mark out circles with cones.

Practice 5

2v2 (+2) Small Sided Game

10 mins

Created using SoccerTutor.com Tactics Manager

Objective
To practice running with the ball, dribbling and finishing on goal (+ beginning to pass).

Description
In this free game we have a 2v2 with 2 extra neutral players that play with the team in possession. The neutral player has unlimited touches like all the other players, but they are not allowed to score.

Change the neutral players often.

Coaching Points
1. This is a free game which should stimulate expression, initiative and the creativity of the players.
2. With a 4v2 situation the players start to learn to use the extra space and time.
3. The aim is to develop their technique and individual tactical play.
4. Encourage players to use the dribbling techniques they have learnt in the 'Technical Block.'

SESSION 10
Practice 1
Ball Control Warm Up - 'Walk in the Forest'   **10 mins**

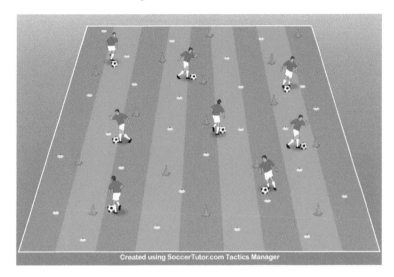

Created using SoccerTutor.com Tactics Manager

Technical objective: Ball control in limited space with obstacles - stopping and turning.

Motor Skills Objective: Running and turning.

Description
The players will pretend to be walking through a forest with lots of flowers (cones) and trees (traffic cones). Players will move around in a square 15 yards x 15 yards with the ball in at their feet (can start with ball in hands), paying attention not to step on the flowers and trees. Every 30 seconds the coach will add more flowers and trees inside the forest, making it harder to walk.

Variations
1. The players can be divided into 2 teams, with one team at a time running onto the pitch within a set time. The team that steps on the least cones win the game.
2. Play in a 10 yards x 10 yards area with only 4 players. The players waiting for their turn dribbles outside the square in a pre-set circuit.

Coaching Points
1. Concentrate on the pace and correction of execution (demonstrate well).
2. Pay attention not to correct with too much persistence, letting the game flow regularly.

Practice 2 - The Technical Block   **15 mins**
See Pages 28-31

Practice 3

Dribbling in an Oval Track - 'Forest Fruits Game' 10 mins

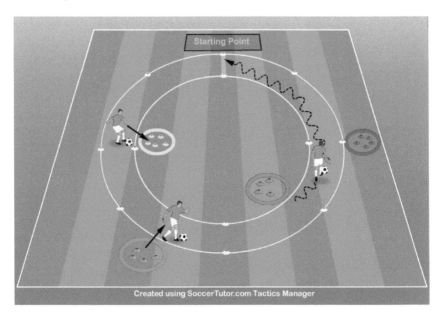

Technical objective: Running with the ball and stopping (control/mastery).

Motor Skills Objective: Running, coordination, reactions, balance & quickness of execution.

Description

This is a competition between 2 teams in a square of 20 yards x 20 yards. An oval track is built with cones and outside there are some harvesting areas. Inside the areas there are yellow cones (bananas), orange cones (oranges), red cones (strawberries) and blue cones (blueberries).

At the start the players will be assigned specific tasks, such as pick up 10 fruits – 3 blueberries, 1 strawberry, 2 bananas and 4 oranges.

The players have a set amount of time to collect all the fruits in the right quantity. Each player can only pick up 1 fruit at a time and take it to the starting point where the coach collects the harvest.

If a player dribbles outside of the track they will have to leave the fruit and go back to the starting point. The coach will record how many fruits the team got and then the other team will have the same time to try and beat them.

Coaching Points
1. This game stimulates the cooperation between the players, so encourage teamwork.
2. Players will need soft touches to stay within the circuit and good control to stop the ball with the sole and reach the 'fruits.'

Practice 4

Shooting Accuracy Game - 'Catch the Rabbits' **15 mins**

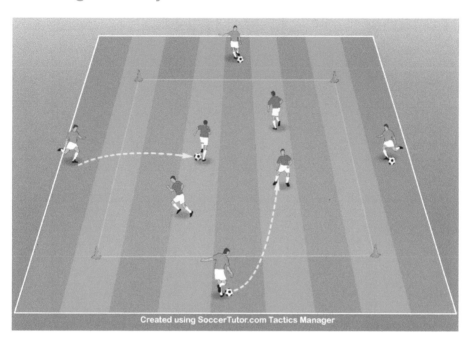

Created using SoccerTutor.com Tactics Manager

Technical objective: Ball striking accuracy.

Motor Skills Objective: Running, throwing, kicking, coordination and awareness of space.

Description
In an area 15 yards x 15 yards, we have a smaller square inside it (10 yards x 10 yards). 4 rabbits will move inside the smaller square and the 4 hunters will try to hit them by throwing a ball from outside (in the larger square).

Then progress to the players kicking the ball to hit the 'rabbits.' Every 1.5 minutes the players will change roles. Be sure to keep the ball on the ground.

Coaching Points
1. At first, require the players to use different methods of throwing the ball.
2. When we progress make sure to demonstrate the correct technique when striking the ball - the head should be over the ball and the non-striking foot should be placed next to the ball when shooting.

Practice 5

2v2 (+2) with 2 Side Zones in a Small Sided Game **10 mins**

Created using SoccerTutor.com Tactics Manager

Objective

To practice dribbling and finishing on goal with the beginning elements of passing (especially to the wide neutral players).

Description

In this free game we have a 2v2 with 2 extra neutral players that play with the team in possession. The neutral players are outside the playing area on the sides and can move freely all the way up and down. They have unlimited touches like all the other players, but they can only keep the ball for 4 seconds before having to pass the ball and are not allowed to score.

Change the neutral players often.

Coaching Points

1. This is a free game which should stimulate expression, initiative and the creativity of the players.
2. Encourage the players to take each other on and run into space to score.
3. The aim is to develop their technique and individual tactical play.
4. Encourage players to use the dribbling techniques they have learnt in the 'Technical Block.'

CHAPTER

6

SESSION 11..80
1. Dribbling Warm Up - 'Learn the Names'...............................80
2. Individual Tactics Block..80
3. 1v1 Duels - 'The Guardian' 81
4. Shooting Practice - '10 Pin Bowling'................................82
5. 4v4 with 'End Zones' in a Small Sided Game.......................83

SESSION 12..84
1. Warm Up - 'Moving Basket Game'....................................84
2. Individual Tactics Block 84
3. 1v1 Duels with Gates - 'The Chase'................................85
4. Shooting Target Practice - 'The Hole'.............................86
5. 4v4 with 4 Goals in a Small Sided Game...........................87

SESSION 13..88
1. Motor Aerobic Warm Up - 'Fantasy Track' 88
2. Individual Tactics Block..88
3. 1v1 Duels Team Game - 'Capture the Flag' 89
4. Speed Ring Relay Game - 'Reach the Finish Line' 90
5. 4v4 with 6 Goals in a Small Sided Game............................91

SESSION 14..92
1. 1v1 Warm Up - 'The Battle'...92
2. Individual Tactics Block..92
3. Technical Feints / Moves to Beat - 'The Tunnel' 93
4. Jump, Dribble and Shoot - 'The Tracks'............................94
5. 4v4 with 4 Goals in a Small Sided Game...........................95

SESSION 15..96
1. 6v2 Dribble and Tag Game - 'The Fisherman'.......................96
2. Individual Tactics Block..96
3. 1v1 Duels Team Game - 'The Net' 97
4. Motor Aerobic Dribbling Game - 'The Dolphin' 98
5. 4v4 with 4 Dribble Gates in a Small Sided Game 99

SESSION 11
Practice 1
Dribbling Warm Up - 'Learn the Names'   10 mins

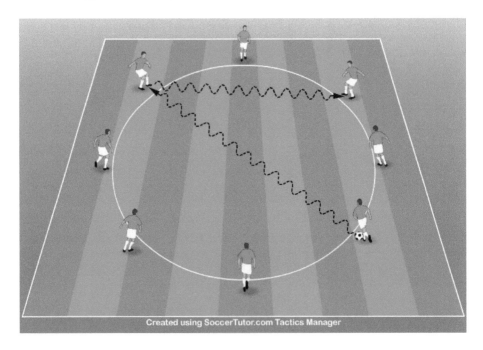

Created using SoccerTutor.com Tactics Manager

Technical objective: Running with the ball and stopping the ball (control/mastery).

Motor Skills Objective: Running, stopping and socialising (communication).

Description
Players are in a circle and one of them has the ball. The players start with their hands and the objective is to carry and then throw the ball to a teammate. They call the player's name first and then take their place. Then progress to dribbling with the ball.

We can then progress again from dribbling the ball to their teammate, to dribbling the ball up to the player and stopping it in front of him.

Coaching Points
1. Get the players to use all different parts of their foot to dribble and stop the ball.
2. Create a positive and fun environment with lots of communication.
3. Stimulate the participation of all the players with an emphasis on socialising.

Practice 2 - Individual Tactics Block   15 mins
See Pages 32-36

Practice 3
1v1 Duels - 'The Guardian'

10 mins

Technical objective: Dribbling and stopping the ball (Ball control) and feints in a game situation.

Motor Skills Objective: Running, coordination, reactions, adapting and quickness of execution

Description
STAGE 1: Set up an area 12 yards x 8 yards. 1 player must run beyond the line which is guarded by the defender (red) without getting tagged. Every time the guardian tags the player, the players exchange roles.

STAGE 2: Once the players are good at using their body to make feints, a ball and a mini-goal is introduced and the players try to score after beating the guardian.

Coaching Points
1. Ask the players to use the feints they practiced in the 'Individual Tactics Block.'
2. Encourage creativity and the challenge of beating the defender.

Practice 4

Shooting Practice – '10 Pin Bowling'

15 mins

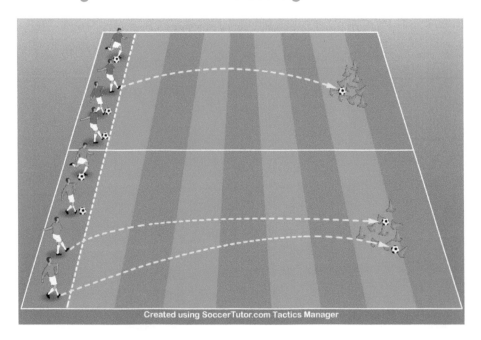

Created using SoccerTutor.com Tactics Manager

Technical objective: To develop the technique for throw-ins and shooting.

Motor Skills Objective: Throw → Kick.

Description

This competitive game is between 2 teams in an area 20 yards x 20 yards. The game is played with the hands at first. On the coach's call, one team must hit as many cones as possible using 1 ball each. Then the other team has their turn.

The team that hits the most cones down get a point.

Variations

1. At first, change the method of throwing; with 1 hand, 2 hands, like a throw-in, etc.
2. When playing with feet vary the part of the foot used; the instep, inside of the foot, etc.

Coaching Points

1. Monitor the correct ball striking technique (head over ball/other foot next to ball).
2. Encourage the competition between the teams to make the practice more fun.

Practice 5

4v4 with 'End Zones' in a Small Sided Game   **10 mins**

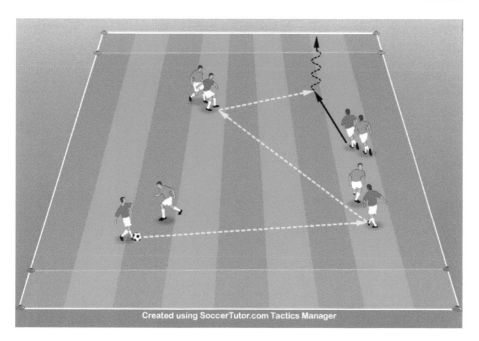

Created using SoccerTutor.com Tactics Manager

Objective
To develop dribbling/stopping the ball and competitive 1v1 play within a team.

Description
Set up mini-fields 20 yards x 20 yards for free games of 4v4.

Players play a game where they score a goal by dribbling the ball through the end zone.

Variation: A goal is scored only if the ball is stopped within the end zone.

Coaching Points
1. This is a free game stimulating the initiative and creativity of the players.
2. This is the beginning of the development of positional play using a light approach.
3. Encourage players to use feints/moves to beat that they have learnt in the 'Individual Tactics Block.'

SESSION 12

Practice 1

Warm Up - 'Moving Basket Game'   **10 mins**

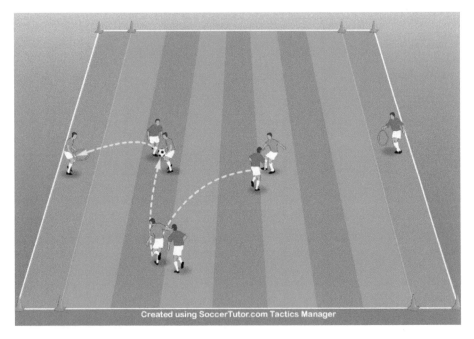

Created using SoccerTutor.com Tactics Manager

Technical objective: Group cooperation and the beginning steps of team play.

Motor Skills Objective: Run → Throw → Catch → Kick.

Description

A game of 3v3 is played in an area of 15 yards x 15 yards. Outside the area, there is 1 player per team holding a ring (the basket). The outside player must move up and down in relation to where the ball is located.

Players play with the hands at first and the objective is to pass the ball to their teammates and to throw the ball in the basket (ring). Then progress to the players kicking the all out of their hands to pass, but they still throw the ball into the 'basket'.

The team that scores more baskets wins the game.

Coaching Points

1. Only progress to kicking the ball if the age/level of the players is suitable.
2. Adapt the rules to the behaviour of the group, encouraging group participation.

Practice 2 - Individual Tactics Block   **15 mins**
See Pages 32-36

Practice 3

1v1 Duels with Gates - 'The Chase'

10 mins

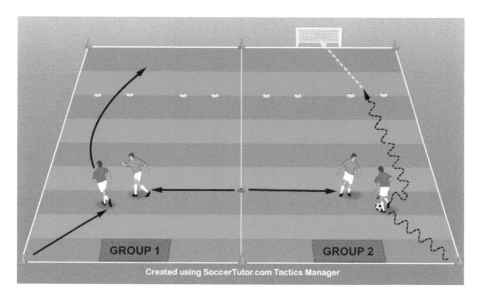

GROUP 1

GROUP 2

Created using SoccerTutor.com Tactics Manager

Technical objective: Feint/moves to beat and dribbling in a 1v1 game situation.

Motor Skills Objective: Running, coordination, reactions, adapting and quickness of execution.

Description

FIELD 1: Set up a an area 12 yards x 8 yards. The attacker (blue) must run through one of the small cone gates without being tagged by the defender (who has started in a position of disadvantage). Assign points.

FIELD 2: Once the players are using the correct body shape to make feints, a ball and a mini-goal are introduced and the players try to score after dribbling through the gates. If the defender tags the player or the ball is lost, they exchange roles.

Variations
1. The coach can call which gate to attack and can change the gate during the play.
2. Older players can progress to tackling instead of tagging.

Coaching Points
1. Focus on running properly and the proper execution of running with the ball.
2. Demonstrate the correct body shape when performing feints/moves to beat.
3. Stimulate creativity, encouraging the challenge and competition.

Practice 4

Shooting Target Practice - 'The Hole'   **15 mins**

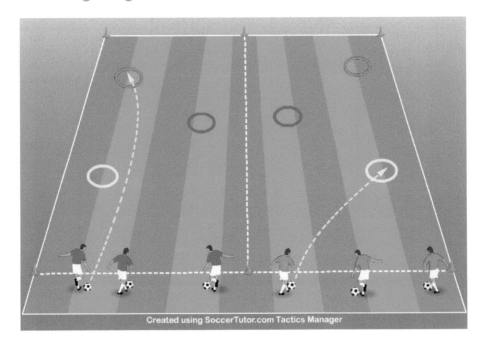

Created using SoccerTutor.com Tactics Manager

Technical objective: To develop the technique for throw-ins and ball striking accuracy.

Motor Skills Objective: Throwing and kicking.

Description

This is a competitive game between 2 teams in an area 20 yards x 20 yards (divided in half). In each half of the field there are some rings placed at various distances. Points will be assigned to each ring (rings further away are assigned the most points).

The game is played with the hands at first. At the coach's command, 1 player per team aims to throw/kick the ball into the ring. The team that scores the most points win the game.

Variations

1.   At first, change the method of throwing; with 1 hand, 2 hands, like a throw-in, etc.
2.   When playing with feet vary the part of the foot used; the instep, inside of the foot, etc.

Coaching Points

1.   Demonstrate and monitor the correct technique for throw-ins and striking with feet.
2.   Create a positive and fun environment & stimulate competition between the teams.

Practice 5

4v4 with 4 Goals in a Small Sided Game

10 mins

Created using SoccerTutor.com Tactics Manager

Objective

To develop dribbling, shooting and competitive 1v1 play within a team.

Description

Set up mini-fields 20 yards x 20 yards for free games of 4v4.

Players play a game where they can score in 2 goals and defend the 2 goals at the other end.

Variation

All payers can score in all 4 goals.

Coaching Points

1. This is a free game stimulating the initiative and creativity of the players.

2. This is the beginning of the development of positional play using a light approach.

3. Encourage players to use feints/moves to beat they have learnt in the 'Individual Tactics Block.'

SESSION 13
Practice 1
Motor Aerobic Warm Up - 'Fantasy Track'　　10 mins

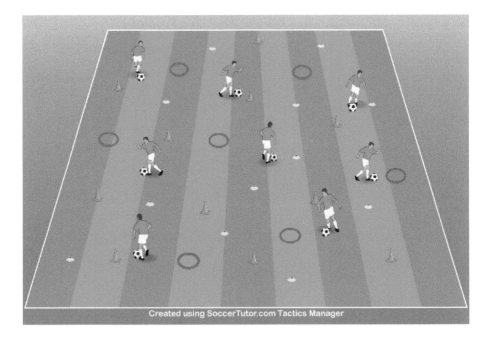

Created using SoccerTutor.com Tactics Manager

Technical objective: Ball control/mastery.

Motor Skills Objective: Running, jumping, crawling, coordination and motor creativity.

Description

Various obstacles are placed in an area 20 yards x 20 yards, such as cones, trafficcones, speed rings etc. The players are asked to run freely around the field and around the obstacles.

We then introduce the balls and ask the players to do everything they want on the field allowing them to dribble, play with their hands, roll, crawl, jump, etc.

Coaching Points
1. Encourage the players to use different parts of the feet when dribbling.
2. Use this exercise to observe the creativity of the players when they are free.

Practice 2 - Individual Tactics Block　　15 mins
See Pages 32-36

Practice 3

1v1 Duels Team Game - 'Capture the Flag'   **10 mins**

Created using SoccerTutor.com Tactics Manager

Technical objective: Ball control/mastery, dribbling and feints/moves to beat in 1v1s.

Motor Skills Objective: Run, coordination, reactions, adapting and quickness of execution.

Description
Players line up at the sides and are assigned a number. The coach places a ball in the centre of the field. The coach calls a number and the 2 players with the same number run to challenge for the ball.

The first player to the ball becomes the attacker and can score in either of the 2 mini-goals. If the player scores, they gets 1 point for their team.

Coaching Points
1. Firstly focus making sure the players are running properly.
2. Encourage the use of dribbling techniques from the 'Technical Block' and feints/moves to beat from the 'Individual Tactics Block.'
3. Stimulate creativity, encouraging the players to challenge and to be competitive.

Practice 4

Speed Ring Relay Game - 'Reach the Finish Line' 15 mins

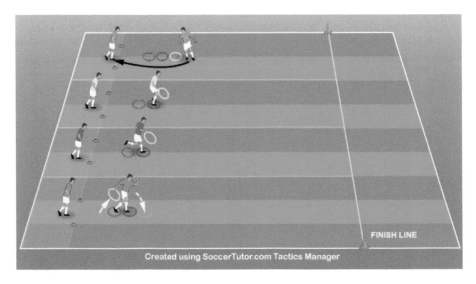

Technical objective: To develop the players coordination skills and teamwork.

Motor Skills Objective: Walking, running, bending down, picking up and jumping.

Description

This is a competitive game between 4 teams in an area of 40 yards x 40 yards (divided into 4 mini-fields). In each section various rings are placed.

On the coach's call, the first player in line will jump inside a ring (or pick it up), grab it, jump over all the other rings and place the ring he holds at the end of the line. Once they drop the ring, they run back to their teammate to high five them.

The line of rings will get closer to the finish line and the team that reaches the finish line first with a ring wins the game.

Variations

Change the type of jumping; with 2 feet, with only 1 foot, right or left.

Coaching Point

1. Create a positive and fun environment and stimulate competition between the teams.

Practice 5

4v4 with 6 Goals in a Small Sided Game

10 mins

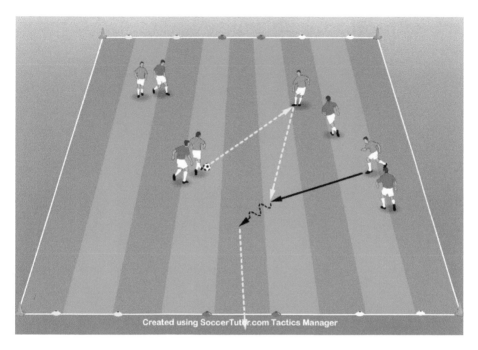

Created using SoccerTutor.com Tactics Manager

Objective
To develop dribbling, shooting and competitive 1v1 play within a team.

Description
Set up mini-fields for free games of 4v4 in an area 20 yards x 20 yards.

Place 3 small goals at both ends (or cone gate goals as shown) with a different colour for each goal. The aim is to score in one of these small goals.

During the game the coach will call a colour indicating the goal the players need to score in or the goal where the players are not allowed to score.

Coaching Points
1. You can keep changing the goal they are aiming to score in to develop concentration and awareness.
2. You can also vary the size of the goals and how many points they are worth.
3. Encourage players to use feints/moves to beat they have learnt in the 'Individual Tactics Block.'

SESSION 14

Practice 1

1v1 Warm Up - 'The Battle'   **10 mins**

Created using SoccerTutor.com Tactics Manager

Technical objective: Ball control/mastery, dribbling and feints/moves to beat in 1v1s.

Motor Skills Objective: Run, coordination, reactions, adapting and quickness of execution.

Description

STAGE 1: In an area 20 yards x 20 yards the players are in pairs and play in 1v1 duels. The game starts without the ball, and 1 player from each pair will have a bib on pretending to have a tail. Players run free inside the field and on the coach's command the other players must try to grab the tail from their direct opponent.

STAGE 2: Players are organised in pairs but this time they dribble the ball. At the coach's command the player with the ball must defend the ball as long as possible while the other player tries to gain possession.

Coaching Points

1. When dribbling the ball the players need to use their body as a barrier between the defending player and the ball (demonstrate this shielding technique).
2. Match players up in similar age/level to make sure the competition is fair.

Practice 2 - Individual Tactics Block   **15 mins**
See Pages 32-36

Practice 3

Technical Feints / Moves to Beat - 'The Tunnel'   **10 mins**

Technical objective: Ball control/mastery, dribbling and feints/moves to beat in 1v1s.

Motor Skills Objective: Run, coordination, reactions, adaptation and quickness.

Description
STAGE 1: In an area 12 yards x 8 yards one player (blue) stands on the line with open legs and the other player dribbles the ball and must pass the ball through the legs of the blue player and then finish with a shot on goal.

STAGE 2: Once the players have mastered the pass under the legs, the other player can become an active defender and will actively defend the goal.

Variation
The defender, instead of waiting without moving, can move their legs open and closed (like star jumps).

Coaching Points
1. Encourage and observe the creativity of the players.
2. Players should use feints/moves to beat they have learnt in the 'Individual Tactics Block.'

Practice 4

Jump, Dribble and Shoot - 'The Tracks'   **15 mins**

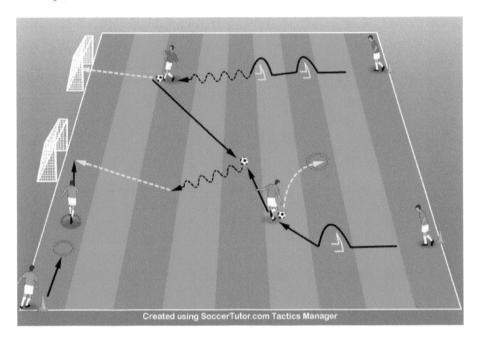

Created using SoccerTutor.com Tactics Manager

Technical objective: Running with the ball (control), ball striking accuracy and throws-Ins.

Motor Skills Objective: Run → Throw → Kick.

Description
Players are organised into 3 teams and start at the same time.

Blue Team: Starting with the ball in their hands, they jump over the hurdles then dribble the ball and finish on goal. They then become defenders and will challenge the red player for the ball in the centre.

Red Team: They jump the obstacle with the ball in their hands, then they throw or kick the ball at the target (ring). They take the ball the coach placed in the centre and dribble trying to finish on goal (challenged by a blue player).

Orange Team: They hop through the rings (placed in any pattern) and become goalkeepers. Every 3 minutes change the roles of the teams.

Coaching Points
1. Make sure not to use hurdles larger than 6 inches for this age group.
2. Throwing or kicking the ball at the target will depend on the age or level of player.
3. If the players are more advanced, you can get them to pass the ball under the hurdles when they are jumping over them.

Practice 5
4v4 with 4 Goals in a Small Sided Game

10 mins

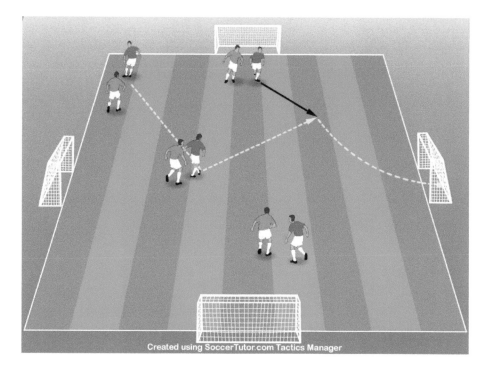

Created using SoccerTutor.com Tactics Manager

Objective
To develop dribbling, shooting and competitive 1v1 play within a team.

Description
Set up mini-fields for free games of 4v4 in an area 20 yards x 20 yards. Goals can be scored in any of the 4 mini goals by players from both teams.

Variation
Assign 2 goals to defend and 2 goals to attack for each team.

Coaching Points
1. Push the players to be creative and demonstrate what they have learnt to try and beat their opponents.
2. Players should dribble the ball with different parts of the foot.
3. Encourage players to use feints/moves to beat they have learnt in the 'Individual Tactics Block.'

SESSION 15
Practice 1
6v2 Dribble and Tag Game - 'The Fisherman'   **10 mins**

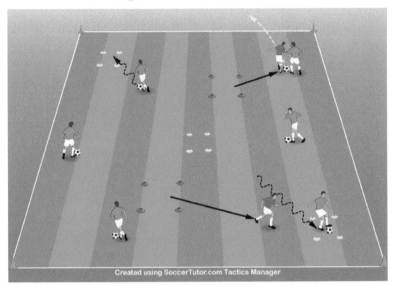

Created using SoccerTutor.com Tactics Manager

Technical objective: Ball control/mastery, dribbling and feints/moves to beat in 1v1s.

Motor Skills Objective: Running, coordination, adaptation and motor reactions.

Description

In an area 20 yards x 20 yards the players (the fish) dribble the ball. On the field there are 2 blue houses (2 x 2 yards) where the fishermen live.

On the coach's call, the fishermen come out of their houses to catch the fish by kicking the ball out of the area. The fish can find shelter in the safe houses (yellow) where they cannot be challenged for 5 seconds.

Variations: 1) Play without the ball. **2)** The fish are caught if they are tagged by the fishermen.

Coaching Points

1. Make sure to enforce the rules, especially the 5 seconds allowed in the safe houses.
2. Players need to use their body to create a barrier between the defender and the ball (shielding).
3. Change the fishermen role often.

Practice 2 - Individual Tactics Block   **15 mins**
See Pages 32-36

Practice 3

1v1 Duels Team Game - 'The Net'

10 mins

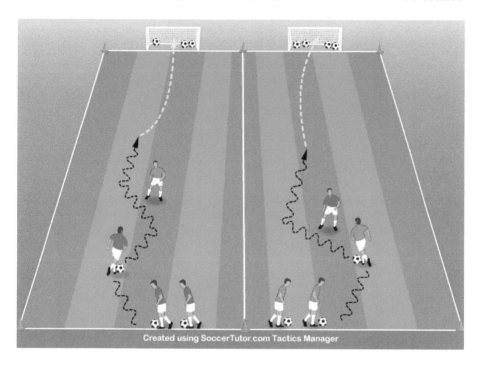

Created using SoccerTutor.com Tactics Manager

Technical objective: Ball control/mastery, dribbling and feints/moves to beat in 1v1s.

Motor Skills Objective: Run, coordination, reactions, adaptation and quickness of execution.

Description
In an area 12 yards x 8 yards, 2 teams play. The game consists of putting as many fish (balls) inside the net (the goal) while avoiding the opposition defender. The second player starts as soon as the first player has taken a shot on goal.

Variation
Use timed games seeing how many goals a team can score.

Coaching Points
1. Stimulate the 1v1 competition, encouraging the use of different parts of the foot and various feints/moves to beat.
2. Monitor the correct technique of the players.
3. Create a positive and fun environment with an emphasis on competition.

Practice 4

Motor Aerobic Dribbling Game - 'The Dolphin' **15 mins**

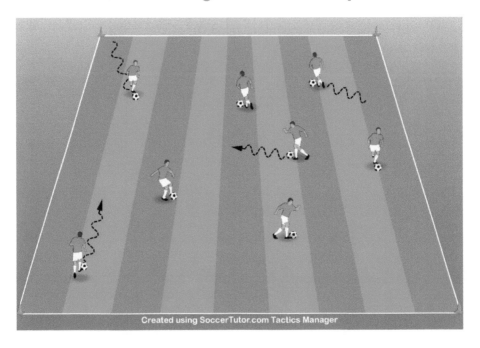

Created using SoccerTutor.com Tactics Manager

Technical objective: Ball control/mastery.

Motor Skills Objective: Running and jumping.

Description
Use an area 12 yards x 12 yards. At first, the players run in the square without the ball. When the coach calls a name of a player, that player becomes the dolphin and must jump over the other players who have laid on the ground.

Once the players are comfortable, do the same but now everyone is dribbling a ball around the square.

Coaching Points
1. Make sure players have good concentration and awareness to avoid collisions.
2. A good progression is for the players to jump with the ball trapped between their feet.

Practice 5

4v4 with 4 Dribble Gates in a Small Sided Game **10 mins**

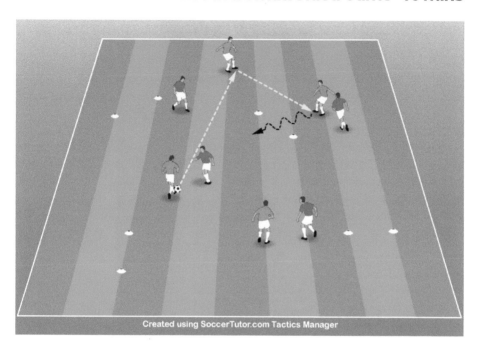

Created using SoccerTutor.com Tactics Manager

Objective
To develop dribbling, shooting and competitive 1v1s along with the beginnings of learning positional play.

Description
Set up 2 mini-fields for free games of 4v4. Place 4 mini goal gates with cones randomly on the field. Goals are scored when a player dribbles through these gates. The goal is valid going through both sides of the goal.

Variation
Do not allow 2 consecutive goals in the same gate.

Coaching Points
1. Push the players to be creative and demonstrate what they have learnt to try and beat their opponents.
2. Players should dribble the ball with different parts of the foot.
3. Encourage players to use feints/moves to beat they have learnt in the 'Individual Tactics Block.'

CHAPTER

7

SESSION 16...101

1. Quick Reactions Dribbling Race - 'The Colours'....................101
2. Individual Tactics Block...101
3. Dribble, Jump and Shoot with Goalkeepers..........................102
4. Run, Jump and Score First with 4 Players 103
5. 4x4 - Free Small Side Game...104

SESSION 17...105

1. Coordination Circuit Training - 'The Numbers'.....................105
2. Individual Tactics Block...105
3. 1v1 Back to Goal Duel - 'Turn and Go'.............................106
4. Football Tennis Game 107
5. 2v2 Zones in a 4v4 Small Sided Game...............................108

SESSION 18...109

1. Ball Control Warm Up - 'The Alphabet'.............................109
2. Individual Tactics Block...109
3. 1v1 Duel with a Goal - 'Lateral Defender' 110
4. Throw, Catch, Run, Jump, Dribble and Shoot.......................111
5. 2v2 Vertical Zones in a 4v4 Small Sided Game......................112

SESSION 19...113

1. Running & Dribbling Warm Up - 'Return Home'.......................113
2. Individual Tactics Block...113
3. 1v1 Frontal Duel with 3 Goals.....................................114
4. Dribbling Multiple Balls / Objects - 'The Move' 115
5. 4v4 with 'Scoring Zones' in a Small Sided Game....................116

SESSION 20...117

1. Turning and Shooting Game - 'World Cup Qualifiers' 117
2. Individual Tactics Block...117
3. Dribble and Shoot - 'Shooting Range'..............................118
4. Jump, Dribble and Shoot - 'Shooting Range (2)' 119
5. 4v4 with 6 Dribble Gates in a Small Sided Game....................120

SESSION 16
Practice 1
Quick Reactions Dribbling Race - 'The Colours' **10 mins**

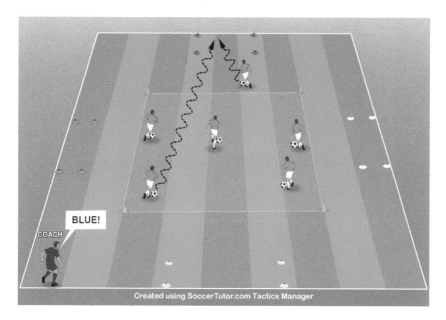

Technical objective: Ball control/mastery and dribbling at speed.

Motor Skills Objective: Running, coordination, adapting and motor reactions.

Description
The players dribble the ball in an area 12 yards x 12 yards. On the outside there are 4 coloured zones. The coach calls a colour and all the players must quickly run towards the coloured zone called out by the coach. The last player to arrive in the zone will be subject to a penalty or lose a point.

Variation: Associate the colour to an object or image, such as 'Lets go to the sea' (blue).

Coaching Points
1. When dribbling within the square players need to use small touches (keeping the ball close to their feet) and have good concentration/awareness to avoid collisions.
2. Make sure the players react quickly to your call, encouraging them to dribble quickly to the correct coloured zone.

Practice 2 - Individual Tactics Block   **15 mins**
See Pages 32-36

Practice 3

Dribble, Jump and Shoot with Goalkeepers   10 mins

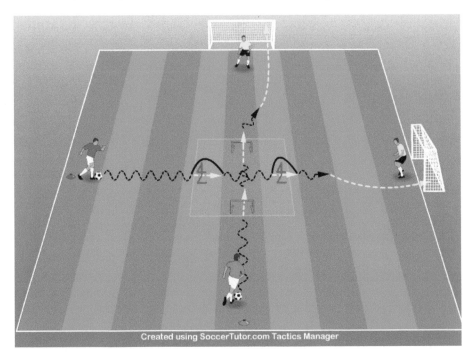

Created using SoccerTutor.com Tactics Manager

Technical objective: Ball control, feints, shooting and developing peripheral vision/ awareness.

Motor Skills Objective: Running, jumping, coordination, adapting and quickness of execution.

Description
We use an area 12 yards x 12 yards and mark out a square using obstacles (low hurdles or tape).

On the coach's call, 2 players dribble the ball at the same time as shown and jump over the hurdles, passing the ball underneath the hurdle, making sure to look up and be aware of the other player to avoid a collision. Then the players shoot on goal where a goalkeeper tries to save the shot.

Variation: Substitute the goalkeeper with a defender and create a 1v1 situation instead.

Coaching Points
1. This practice is very good at stimulating peripheral vision, so keep reminding the players to look up and be aware of their surroundings and their opponent.
2. Encourage creativity, using all parts of the foot to dribble and shoot.
3. Create good competition during this exercise (1 point to the player who scores first).

Practice 4

Run, Jump and Score First with 4 Players **15 mins**

Created using SoccerTutor.com Tactics Manager

Technical objective: Ball control, feints, shooting and developing peripheral vision/awareness.

Motor Skills Objective: Running, jumping, coordination, adapting and quickness of execution.

Description

We use an area 12 yards x 12 yards and mark out a square using obstacles (low hurdles or tape).

On the coach's call, 4 players dribble the ball at the same time as shown and jump over the hurdles, passing the ball underneath the hurdle, making sure to look up and be aware of the other players to avoid a collisions.

The players must shoot in the goal opposite to them (as shown in the diagram).

Coaching Points
1. This practice is even more important for the players to concentrate and show good awareness, so keep reminding the players to look up and be aware of their opponents.
2. Do not use hurdles higher than 6 inches for this age group.
3. Create good competition during this exercise (4 points for scoring first, 3 points for second etc).

Practice 5

4x4 - Free Small Side Game

10 mins

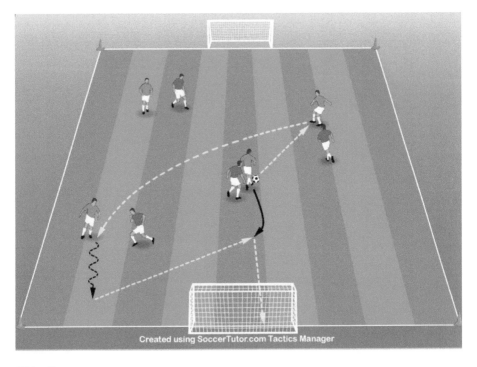

Created using SoccerTutor.com Tactics Manager

Objective
To develop competitive 1v1 play within a team and finishing on goal. This also trains the beginnings of positional play with a light approach.

Description
Set up mini-fields where the players play mini games of 4v4.

Coaching Points
1. This is a free game which should stimulate expression, initiative and the creativity of the players.
2. Encourage the players to take each other on and run into space to score.
3. The aim is to develop their technique and individual tactical play.
4. Encourage players to use feints/moves to beat they have learnt in the 'Individual Tactics Block.'

SESSION 17
Practice 1

Coordination Circuit Training - 'The Numbers' **10 mins**

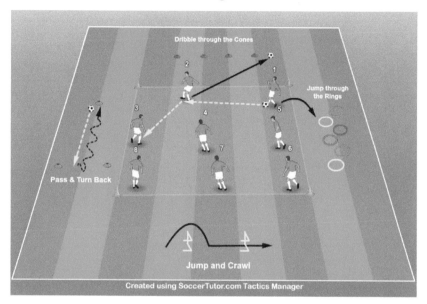

Technical objective: Running with/stopping the ball (control/mastery).

Motor Skills Objective: Run → Jump → Kick. Coordination, adapting and motor reactions.

Description
The players are assigned a number 1 to 8. The players must pass the ball following the sequence of the numbers. Outside the square there are 4 technical/coordination stations that the players must work on quickly after their pass, before running back to the square.

As soon as 1 has passed to 2, he chooses one of the 4 circuits to complete and then quickly runs back to join in the passing sequence again. Ask the players not to go to a station that is occupied by another player. Start the practice with the hands and quickly progress.

Coaching Points
1. Let the players have freedom of initiative for the 4 circuits.
2. The circuits need to be done quickly so the players are back in position in time to play their next pass in the sequence.

Practice 2 - Individual Tactics Block   **15 mins**
See Pages 32-36

Practice 3
1v1 Back to Goal Duel - 'Turn and Go'   **10 mins**

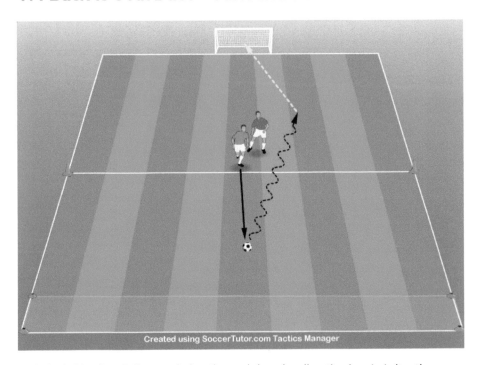

Created using SoccerTutor.com Tactics Manager

Technical objective: Ball control, shooting and changing direction in a 1v1 situation.

Motor Skills Objective: Running, coordination, reactions, adapting and quickness of execution.

Description
In an area 12 yards x 8 yards, players start in the same position in one half, but with 1 player slightly ahead of the other.

The players play a 1v1 with the attacker starting with his back to the goal. The ball is in the other half and both players try to claim the ball. The attacker's aim is to bring the ball under control, dribble past the defender and score in the goal.

If the defender intercepts the ball they must dribble into the end zone on the opposite side and successfully stop the ball within the zone to score a goal.

Coaching Points
1. Stimulate the 1v1 competition, encouraging the use of different parts of the foot and various feints/moves to beat ('Technical Block' and 'Individual Tactics Block').
2. The attacker needs to use their body as a shield in between the defender and the ball. Demonstrate the correct body shape to shield the ball.

Practice 4

Football Tennis Game

15 mins

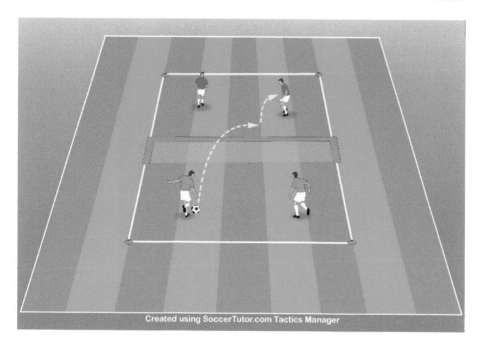

Created using SoccerTutor.com Tactics Manager

Technical objective: Throw-ins and ball striking.

Motor Skills Objective: Throw → Catch → Kick.

Description
Set up mini 'Tennis courts' close to each other. Every court is divided in the middle by a net or tape or cones. The players throw the ball over to the other side. A point is scored when the ball bounces at least twice on the opposition's side.

Progressions
1. Players must catch the ball in the air.
2. Kick the ball out of the hands.

Coaching Points
1. Quickly use the progressions for the older children.
2. For the younger children, kicking out of the hands may be too advanced a skill.
3. Adjust the height of the net depending on the age/level.

Practice 5

2v2 Zones in a 4v4 Small Sided Game

10 mins

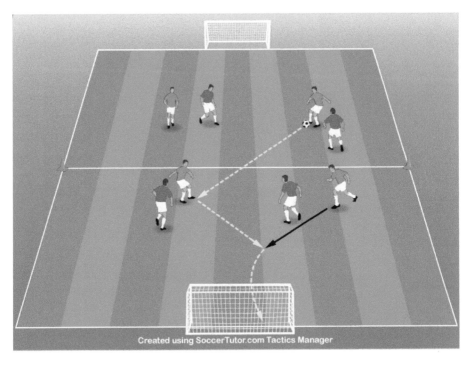

Created using SoccerTutor.com Tactics Manager

Objective

To develop passing, dribbling, shooting and competitive 1v1 play along with the beginning elements of learning about different areas (defending/attacking) and positional play.

Description

In this free game we have a 4v4 situation. In each half we have 2 players from both teams. The players must stay in their half.

The aim is to pass the ball from the defensive half to the attacking half and score a goal. Switch the positions of the players often.

Coaching Points

1. Push the players to be creative and demonstrate what they have learned to try and beat their opponents.

2. Players should dribble the ball with different parts of the foot.

3. Encourage players to use feints/moves to beat they have learnt in the 'Individual

SESSION 18
Practice 1

Ball Control Warm Up - 'The Alphabet'　　　**10 mins**

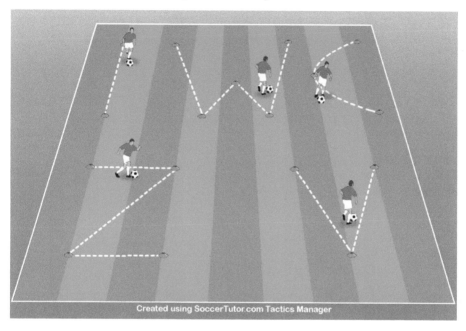

Created using SoccerTutor.com Tactics Manager

Technical objective: Running with the ball (control/mastery) and turning.

Motor Skills Objective: Running with vision and imagery.

Description

Letters of the alphabet are drawn on the field with cones and the players dribble around the letters.

The ball is like a pen and the players must draw out the shape of the letters, performing different changes of direction depending on what letter they are drawing.

Coaching Points

1. Concentrate on the various ways to run/dribble with the ball,
2. Encourage the players to stay as close as possible to the outline of the letters, with the ball close to their feet using small touches.
3. Create a positive and fun environment with the players imagining they are drawing.

Practice 2 - Individual Tactics Block　　　**15 mins**
See Pages 32-36

Practice 3

1v1 Duel with a Goal - 'Lateral Defender'   **10 mins**

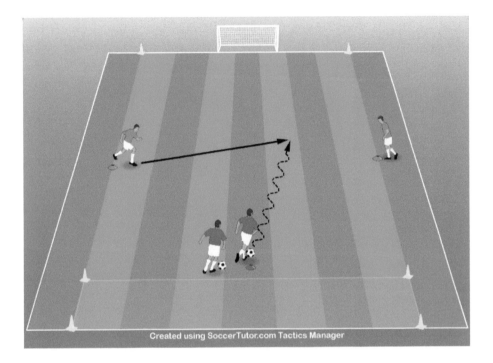

Created using SoccerTutor.com Tactics Manager

Technical objective: Ball control, feints and changes of direction in a 1v1 game situation.

Motor Skills Objective: Running, coordination, reactions, adapting and quickness of execution.

Description

In an area 12 yards x 8 yards, 2 teams play. The blue players dribble the ball with the objective to shoot on goal, while avoiding the challenge of the defender that is coming from the side (red).

Both players set off from their respective positions at the same time. The attacking team aim to beat the defender and score in the goal.

Variation: If the defender wins the ball they can dribble into the end zone to score.

Coaching Points

1. Encourage the use of feints/moves to beat from the 'Individual Tactics Block.'
2. Creativity should be displayed with players using all parts of both feet.
3. When the defender wins the ball they should use the sole of their foot to stop the ball in the 'End Zone.'

Practice 4

Throw, Catch, Run, Jump, Dribble and Shoot **15 mins**

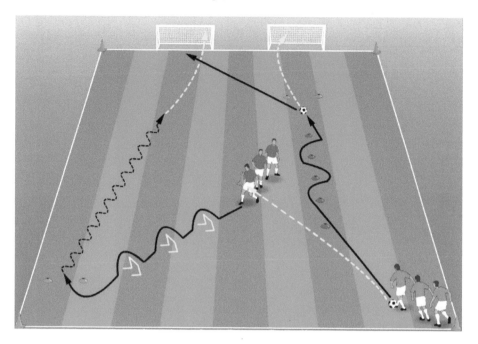

Technical objective: Running with the ball (control/mastery), throw-ins, and shooting.

Motor Skills Objective: Run → Throw → Catch → Kick → Jump → Coordination.

Description

RED PLAYERS: They start by either rolling, throwing or passing the ball to the blue player in the centre. After the pass they run in and out of the cones, and shoot the ball in the goal at the end (where the coach has placed the ball). After their shot, they move to become the goalkeeper in the other goal.

BLUE PLAYERS: Once they receive the ball from the red player, they must carry the ball and jump over the hurdles (or crawl), run around the cone and quickly dribble forwards and shoot at goal against the red goalkeeper.

Variations: 1) Change the motor exercises (jump, roll, crawl). **2)** Blues run through the cones with a ball. **3)** Vary the distances of the cones.

Coaching Points
1. Vary how much the players use their feet in this practice or whether they jump/crawl with the hurdles etc. depending on their age/level.

Practice 5

2v2 Vertical Zones in a 4v4 Small Sided Game   **10 mins**

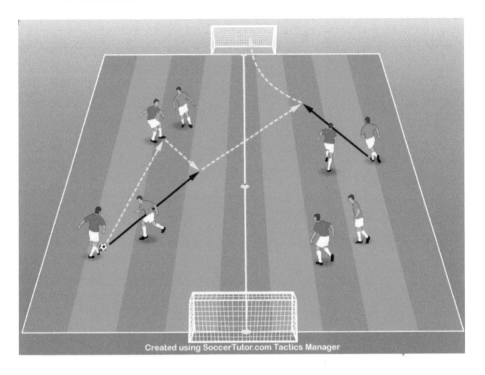

Created using SoccerTutor.com Tactics Manager

Objective

To develop dribbling and shooting in competitive 1v1 situations, along with the beginning elements of passing and learning about different areas (defending/attacking) with positional play.

Description

In this small sided game we play 4v4. We divide the pitch vertically as shown and we have a 2v2 situation in each half.

The players are not allowed to enter the other half.

Coaching Points

1. Push the players to be creative and demonstrate what they have learnt to try and beat their opponents.

2. Players should dribble the ball with different parts of the foot.

3. Encourage players to use feints/moves to beat they have learnt in the 'Individual Tactics Block.'

SESSION 19
Practice 1
Running & Dribbling Warm Up - 'Return Home' **10 mins**

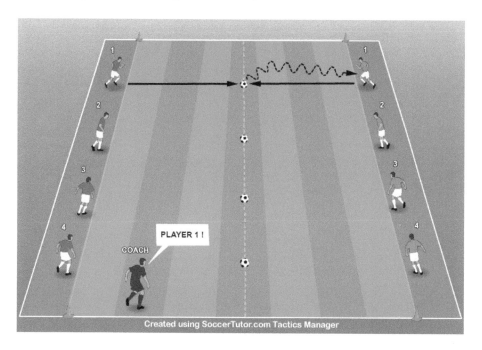

Created using SoccerTutor.com Tactics Manager

Technical objective: Running with/stopping the ball (control/mastery), feints/moves to beat and dribbling in a 1v1 situation.

Motor Skills Objective: Running, coordination, adapting and motor reactions.

Description
Each player is assigned a number. When the coach calls a number the players battle for the ball that is directly in front of them.

The player who gets to the ball first and brings it home gets a point for the team. Players cannot enter their opponent's side of the pitch.

Variation: The opponents can enter the opponent's half and if they touch the ball it is a draw.

Coaching Point
1. Create a positive and fun environment, stimulating competition and creativity.

Practice 2 - Individual Tactics Block   **15 mins**
See Pages 32-36

Practice 3
1v1 Frontal Duel with 3 Goals

10 mins

Created using SoccerTutor.com Tactics Manager

Technical objective: Running with the ball (control/mastery) and changing direction in 1v1s.

Motor Skills Objective: Running, coordination, reactions, adapting and quickness of execution.

Description
In an area 10 yards x 10 yards, we have a 1v1 situation. 1 player starts with the ball and can score in any of the 3 goals.

The defender must challenge the player and if they win the ball they can also score in any of the 3 goals. This stimulates creativity and quick turning/changes of direction.

Variation: The players have to stop the ball on the line of the goal to score.

Coaching Points
1. In 1v1 situations, players need to shield the ball making their body a barrier between the ball and the defender.
2. Reactions are key because if you lose the ball, you have to quickly move to win it back before the opponent can score.
3. Encourage creativity, with both players using all parts of both feet to dribble withand using the feints/moves to beat from the 'Individual Tactics Block.'

Practice 4

Dribbling Multiple Balls / Objects – 'The Move'   **15 mins**

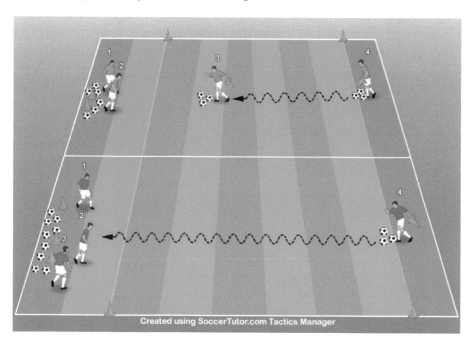

Created using SoccerTutor.com Tactics Manager

Technical objective: Dribbling (ball control/mastery) with an emphasis on speed.

Motor Skills Objective: Walk → Run → Carry → Stop.

Description

The teams must organise themselves in bringing the various objects from one side of the field to the other.

In this example the players are asked to transport 3 balls and one traffic cone at the same time to the teammates on the other side of the field. Play the game as a relay game and the team that finishes first wins.

Variation: Transport various different objects (sticks, balls, cones, rings, hurdles etc).

Coaching Points

1. The speed of play is important here as it is a competition, but the main focus should be on keeping good control of the balls/objects.
2. Demonstrate for the players how best to transport various items.
3. Players should use both feet and different parts of the foot when dribbling.

Practice 5

4v4 with 'Scoring Zones' in a Small Sided Game **10 mins**

Created using SoccerTutor.com Tactics Manager

Objective

To practice and develop techniques for dribbling and shooting within a team/game situation.

Description

This is a free game of 4v4. There are 2 End Zones in which the defending team are not allowed to enter. The team in possession aim to dribble in or pass to a teammate in the End Zone.

If the player successfully receives and controls the ball in the zone, they are free to shoot on goal unopposed.

Coaching Points

1. Push the players to be creative and demonstrate what they have learned to try and beat their opponents.

2. Players should dribble the ball with different parts of the foot.

3. Encourage players to use feints/moves to beat they have learnt in the 'Individual Tactics Block.'

SESSION 20
Practice 1
Turning and Shooting Game - 'World Cup Qualifiers'

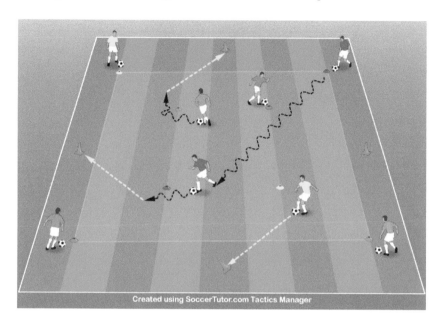

Technical objective: Ball control, changes of direction and accurate ball striking (shooting).

Motor Skills Objective: Running, coordination, motor reactions and quickness of execution.

Description
4 teams of 2-3 players are formed to compete in the world cup tournament. The qualifying games will assign points that will be accumulated with the points of the following games.

The first players of each team start at the same time and dribble the ball around the cone opposite to them (as shown in the diagram). Once they have gone around the cone they must hit one of the cones placed on the outside of the square.

The team that hits a cone first gets 2 points, the second team gets 1 point. As soon as the player shoots at the cone, the next player can go.

Coaching Points
1. Create a positive, fun environment encouraging competition and speed of play.

Practice 2 - Individual Tactics Block   **15 mins**
See Pages 32-36

Practice 3

Dribble and Shoot – 'Shooting Range'   **10 mins**

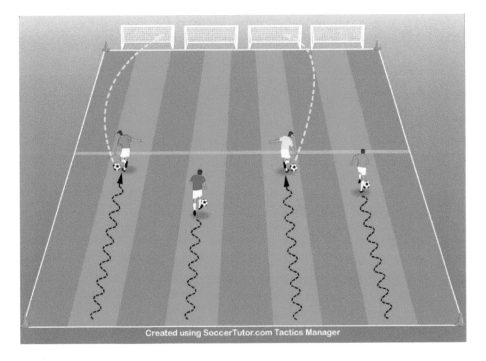

Created using SoccerTutor.com Tactics Manager

Technical objective: Running with the ball (control/mastery), feints, dribbling and SHOOTING.

Motor Skills Objective: Running, kicking and quickness of execution.

Description
We carry on our world cup tournament here with the 4 teams competing in a shooting game.

The objective is to dribble the ball to the line and then shoot in the goal directly in front of them. Each goal is worth 1 point.

Variations: 1) Passing and then shooting. **2)** Dribbling around cones and then shooting.

Coaching Points
1. When shooting, the non-striking foot should be placed next to the ball.
2. The head should be over the ball and the back straight.
3. When dribbling up to the line, the players need to push the ball forwards so they can step up to the ball to shoot.

Practice 4

Jump, Dribble and Shoot – 'Shooting Range (2)' **15 mins**

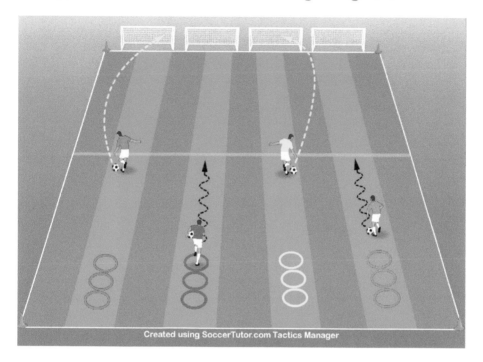

Created using SoccerTutor.com Tactics Manager

Technical objective: Running with the ball (control/mastery), feints, dribbling and *SHOOTING*.

Motor Skills Objective: Running, jumping, crawling, kicking and quickness of execution.

Description

With the same rules as in the previous practice, our 4 teams continue the world cup tournament with another shooting game.

The objective is to jump over the rings while carrying the ball and then dribble the ball up to the line again to shoot in the goal.

Variations

1. Roll over the rings.
2. Throw/catch the ball, then jump over the rings.

Coaching Points

1. The players should take shorter steps up to the ball when preparing to shoot.
2. Create a fun environment and encourage competition between the teams.

Practice 5

4v4 with 6 Dribble Gates in a Small Sided Game **10 mins**

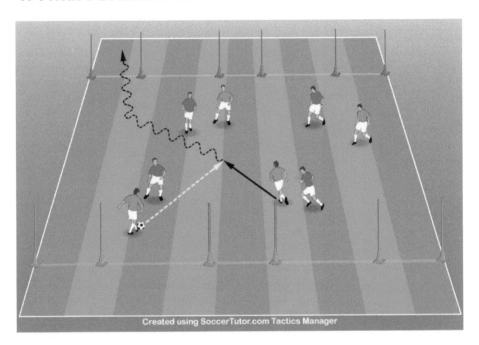

Created using SoccerTutor.com Tactics Manager

Objective
To develop the technique for dribbling and feints/moves to beat in competitive 1v1 play within a team.

Description
We have 3 goals at each end. To score a goal, players have to dribble the ball through one of the gates and stop the ball with the sole of the foot beyond the goal.

Coaching Points
1. This is a free game which should stimulate expression, initiative and the creativity of the players.
2. Encourage the players to take each other on and run into space to score.
3. The aim is to develop their technique and individual tactical play.
4. Encourage players to use the dribbling techniques they have learnt in the 'Technical Block.'

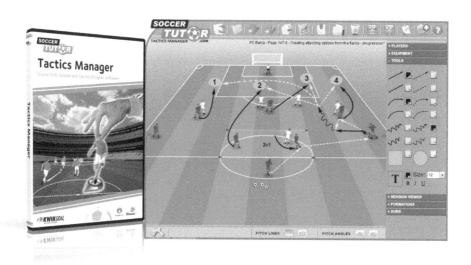

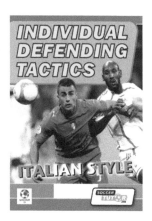